MAKING YOUR MIND MAGNIFICENT

Use the New Brain Science to Transform Your Life: End Negative Thinking, Improve Focus and Clarity, and Be Happier

Steven Campbell, MMIS

Making Your Mind Magnificent

Use the New Brain Science to Transform Your Life: End Negative Thinking, Improve Focus and Clarity, and Be Happier

Steven Campbell
4407 Graywhaler Lane
Rohnert Park, CA 94928

Intelligent Heart Press
www.AnIntelligentHeart.net

ISBN: 978-0-692328-30-9

Dedication

To my beautiful wife, Mary: Thank you for always believing in me. It is that belief, and the love we have for each other, that enabled me to write this book.

To our children, Abigail and Sarah: Your lives have always been an inspiration to me, both the good times and the hard times. What I have learned through you is your greatest gift.

To my mother: The best mother I could ever ask for. You have always been there for me.

To you, the reader: It is such an honor to help you make your mind magnificent!

Contents

Introduction

While I am talking to you, you are talking to yourself three times faster. When I stop talking, you talk to yourself six times faster.

We call this constant conversation your *self-talk*. This self-talk determines *how you see yourself* (called your "self-image"). And...you do not have one self-image, you have thousands: how you see yourself as an athlete, a teacher, a husband, a wife, and so on.

Why am I beginning this Introduction with this little piece of information? Because research has discovered that your brain accepts what you are telling yourself *without question*! No arguments! So when you say, "No way! I can't do that!" the mind simply says, "OK...you can't!" and then blocks out the ways for you to do it. If, however, you say: "Absolutely...of *course* I can do that!" the brain also *accepts* this as truth without question. No arguments. Not only that, your brain then endeavors to help you find a way to do it, and then gives you the energy to do so.

The kicker, however, is that your brain does not *like* change. It does not like being out of its comfort zone. It will resist any changes you want as much as it can, and will find all sorts of ways of doing so, including lying to you and telling you things about yourself that are simply not true.

There's good news, though: Your brain can be taught how to embrace change, and thus become your greatest motivator and friend; to become, as I like to say, your magnificent mind.

This book shows you how.

I have been delivering this information through various presentations and workshops for years now. Invariably at the end of a workshop, a student will ask me why this information wasn't taught 40 years ago. I simply tell them that we did not know then what we know now. In fact, as recently as 30 years ago, the brain was still considered a "black box" and there was little hope of ever determining how it worked. What has changed? Through the explosion in technology such as Magnetic Resonance Imaging (MRI) and Positron Emission Tomography (PET), we have discovered astonishing insights about the brain and learning. Plus, there are simply more of us studying the brain as well. In 1969, the International Society of Neuroscience had 400 registered neuroscientists. As of 2006, its membership numbered 37,000! Jeri Janowsky, a top memory neuroscientist at Oregon Health Sciences University in Portland, says, "Anything you learned two years ago is already old information…Neuroscience is exploding."[1]

This book is based on cutting-edge research that has happened during the past 30 years.

Why teach how your brain works? Because if you cannot understand your brain, you cannot guide it, so instead of shaping your own life, your brain ends up doing most of the shaping. And then you end up feeling like a victim or passenger in life, instead of the driver of your own distinctive existence and untapped potential.[2]

So, through the wonderful discoveries that fill this book, you now have a guidebook in your hand that teaches how to make your mind your greatest motivator and mentor; your wise and trusted counselor and friend. In other words, your brain can now consistently work for you, not against you! And by the end of this book, you will indeed know how to make your mind magnificent.

How to Get the Most Out of This Book

The brain likes to learn in little "chunks," so I have divided the information here into 20 short chapters. I recommend that you read them at your own speed, as the information you will be learning and the insight you will be gaining should not be rushed. The brain really does need time to digest new information. At the end of each chapter there are a few questions to help you apply this material to your own life. After all, that is what this book is all about!

I have been teaching these seminars to college students for years and have seen wonderful changes in my students. When I retired, I began teaching the same information to other audiences, and have seen even more <u>wonderful</u> changes, especially in terms of what people say to themselves all day long. You truly can learn how to make your mind your greatest motivator and friend.

The information from this book comes from a plethora of psychological books and studies, and you will find reference numbers (in superscript) throughout the text.

CHAPTER ONE:

Your Magnificent Min [a]

● ●

"We are fearfully and wonderfully made."
Psalms 139:14

You Want To Change and Grow

The reason you are reading this book is that you want to learn and grow and change. Most of us do. It's a trait deeply ingrained within all of us. The reason learning and change can be so difficult is because your brain *does not want to change*. In fact, as we will learn, research has discovered that your brain's job is to *keep you* from changing. This is why New Year's resolutions seldom work, or why that habit you have been trying to break for years still crops up...either occasionally...or sometimes far more than that.

---

[a]The "mind" is defined in a human as the element or process that reasons, thinks, feels, wills, perceives, judges, etc. The "brain" is defined as the part of the central nervous system enclosed in the cranium of humans and other vertebrates, consisting of a soft, convoluted mass of gray and white matter and serving to control and coordinate the mental and physical actions. This book emphasizes the human element of how we think, learn, grow, and change, rather than the biological aspect of man, I will be therefore be using the term "mind" more than "brain." However, I will at times be using both.

The challenge then is to get your brain to change. You see, the change must begin on the inside, not on the outside. This is why I have written this book: To teach you that your brain cannot only change, but it can become your mentor: A wise and trusted counselor and teacher. This book will help you keep your brain continually on *your* side…so it is always working *for* you and not against you.

What Do I Mean by the "Brain?"

True brains are largely associated with mammals. In addition, their size and complexity tends to be directly related to their specific survival needs.[3] In other words, a herd animal such as a cow has less brain resources than a deer—which must be far more alert.

Humans, on the other hand, have no "standard" way of living. We are the jack-of-all-trades of mammals, extremely adaptable and dependent on the great number of behaviors ¬and a way of living that demands a stupendously large brain. This jack-of-all-trades is the primary reason that humans may properly be regarded as brain freaks. (We regard a giraffe as a neck freak, or an elephant as a nose freak.) The human brain remains the most complex structure in the known universe. It is millions, if not billions of times, more complex than the organ possessed by most other creatures with brains.[4] It never turns off, even in deep sleep. Although it takes up about 2 percent of your body weight, it uses 20 percent of your energy. It also uses 20 percent of the air you breathe, 25 percent of your total blood flow, 30 percent of your water, and 40 percent of the nutrients from your blood.[5] In fact, it uses more of your energy in a 24-hour period than your largest muscles.

Your brain is fully capable of reading the little black squiggles on this piece of bleached wood and deriving meaning from them. To accomplish this miracle, your brain sends jolts of electricity crackling through hundreds of miles of wires composed of brain cells so small that thousands of them could fit into the period at the end of this sentence. Indeed, you are doing that right now! What is equally incredible, given our intimate association with it, is this: None of us have any idea how the brain actually works.[6]

How Much Do We Actually Know About How the Brain Works?

The best way to answer that question is by looking at a comment by Christof Koch, a professor at Caltech, who is known for being among the first in his field to try to figure out how the brain produces consciousness. He tells a tale involving Caenorhabditis elegans, a very small soil-dwelling worm that is famous for being one of the best understood animals on the planet. The nervous system of this little worm consists of only a few hundred neurons, and all of them now have been charted out in great detail. "We have a complete wiring diagram," Dr. Koch writes, but, "We *still have no idea how it works; no overall view of just how the animal functions.*"

The biological structure of the neuron, as is true of any cell in our body, is amazing. Most look just like fried eggs. The white of the egg is the called the 'cytoplasm'; the center yolk is the nucleus. Each of the 10 to 100 trillion cells in our body (as you can see, we still don't really know how many we have) contains a master blueprint called DNA—nearly six feet of the stuff in each cell. This is like putting 30 miles of fishing line and stuffing it into a blueberry. The nucleus is a crowded place.[7]

So...we are just beginning to understand the brain's workings. But do we know enough to make it our ally?

Can the Brain Actually Change?

Absolutely! How's that for a direct answer?

Eric Kandel is the scientist mostly responsible for determining how the brain changes. For his work, he shared the Nobel Prize in 2000. He showed that when people learn something, the wiring in their brains changes. He demonstrated that acquiring even simple pieces of information involves the physical alteration of the structure of the neurons participating in this process. Talking broadly, these physical changes result in the reorganization of the brain. This is astonishing. The brain is constantly learning things, so the brain is constantly rewiring itself.[8]

How do we know? Because the brain uses the outside world to constantly undergo physical and chemical changes as it responds to its environment. This is called plasticity, and it is a startling departure from the old concept of the brain as a self-contained, hard-wired unit that learns from a preset, unchangeable set of rules.[9]

How much can the brain change? There is almost no limit! We know this by looking at its structure and capacity.

The Structure of the Brain

The key cell of the brain is the *neuron*, and the number of neurons we have is beyond astounding! And it seems that the more we study the brain, the more neurons we seem to find. In 1983, Leslie Hart wrote a book titled *Human Brain and Human Learning*. There he cited the research's estimate at 10 to 12 billion neurons. He then says, "I prefer a compromised figure to use as some sort of guide: 30 billion."

The latest research offers an estimated number of 100 billion neurons![10]

But this is nothing! Each of these neurons has an average of 10,000 connections to other neurons. This computes to 100,000,000,000 [10,000] connections! That is a quantity found by multiplying 100 billion, times 100 billion, times 100 billion...ten thousand times. As a comparison, 100 billion multiplied by 40,000 is a number larger than the number of stars in the Milky Way. We truly cannot fathom the number of connections our brain has.

Those connections are used in learning and changing!

In addition, neuroscientists are discovering that there are brain centers for just about everything. There is one for the happiness you experience when you solve a puzzle;[11] there is one for the desire to punish people who cheat to get ahead;[12] there is one for that relates to spiritual experience,[13] and there is one that can turn you from a procrastinator into a workaholic.

So do our brains have an incredible capacity to change? Absolutely!

"But Steve, I've heard that when brain cells die, they don't get replaced. That must be why I am becoming more and more forgetful!"

100 billion neurons is a huge number. It is so big that if 100,000 neurons died every day from the day you were born until the day you reached 80 years old without being replaced (which by the way…a lot of them are!), you will still have 97 percent of them left.[15] We therefore no longer need to worry about how many of our neurons are dying.

The Australian Neurology Nobel Laureate Sir John Eccles said in a lecture at the University of Colorado in 1974 that, "The brain indicates its powers are endless."[16]

In England, John Lorber did autopsies on hydrocephalics. This illness causes all but the 1/6th inch layer of brain tissue to be dissolved by acidic spinal fluid. He tested the IQ's of patients before and during the disease. His findings showed that their IQ remained constant up to death. Although over 90 percent of brain tissue was destroyed by the disease, it had no impact on what we consider to be normal intelligence.

Russian neurosurgeon Alexandre Luria proved that the bulk of frontal lobes (approximately one-third) are mostly dormant. He did this by performing lobotomy experiments where he gave physiological and psychological tests before, cut out parts and whole frontal lobes, then re-tested after. His conclusion: Removal of part or all of frontal lobes causes no major change in brain function, (some change in mood alteration). The frontal lobes are mostly dormant, *asleep*.[17]

The Brain is Not a Computer!

The explosion of computers in the past 50 years has made it very chic to equate the brain with the computer. It has become especially tempting to liken the billions of neurons with the billions of transistors in large computers. More contemporary versions involve the number of nodes in the World Wide Web, or perhaps the number of pages indexed by Google. These huge quantities are also compared to the 100 billion neurons in the brain.

Wrong! After closer examination, the similarity immediately falls apart! In fact, when you have even the briefest conversation with a neurobiologist, the people actually studying neurons, you realize how misleading this comparison becomes.

Transistors in a computer simply switch on and off. Each of the 100 billion neurons (made up of an axon, a myelin sheath, and as many as 15,000 dendrites and synapses) contains a small universe of complexity on both the cellular and microbiological level. Most people understand that neurons signal to one another across synapses through a complicated sequence that involves conversations between electrical and chemical energy, and then back again. However...the signals are themselves affected by cascades of hormones, neurotransmitters, and other chemical modifiers—including the caffeine that we use to keep moving.

Lee Gomes summarized it best in a *Wall Street Journal* article:

> "*These days, it's getting harder to find anyone in cognitive sciences who still believes computers are useful models for intelligence, consciousness and the like. Instead, most people in the field spend their time studying actual brains: Scanning 'em, slicing 'em, dicing 'em. It's essentially the Dreyfus-Searle research agenda: To understand the mind, forget about computers and look at the gray stuff inside our heads.*"[18]

Changing Your Self-Talk

We will discover that what we believe about ourselves is *far more important* than what we do. It is for this reason that all meaningful and lasting growth must start on the inside...with our mind. And we have just learned in this chapter that your brain has almost limitless potential for change and growth...and the more we discover about its capacity, the more we are able to use it as our motivator.

So...your very simple assignment for this chapter is to immediately throw away any notions that you are too old, or too young, or too uneducated, or too stuck in your ways to change. You can grow and change *as much as you want to*! How exciting!!! We no longer need to think of ourselves as limited in terms of how much we can learn, grow, and change. We simply need to know how to do so. That is what this book will teach.

Next Chapter Preview

We have learned how *magnificent* our mind is. We will see this even more as we discover how the brain learns. This is *so* important to understand because it will provide the foundation for understanding how *you* learn; not only in school but how you learn in life, and more specifically, how you learn about yourself.

Remnants to Remember

We have learned two primary principles in this chapter. They are:

1. The brain has an almost infinite capacity to learn, grow and change.
2. The human brain is the most complex structure in the universe.

A Point to Ponder: Getting the Most Value from this Book

Your brain acts as the connection between you and the world. Its job is to continually bring information in, and then endeavor to make sense of it. In other words, it is continually learning.

A tool for validating that learning is through writing. So at the end of every chapter, there will be some very simple questions under Points to Ponder which will involve not only writing down your answers, but also writing down your feelings. As you will learn, what you are thinking and learning is intimately connected to what you are feeling.

By writing down the answers and feelings to these questions, the content of this book will become a cherished part of your life.

Finally, when doing these exercises, trust the first answer that comes to mind. It is usually the most correct.

1. What beliefs do I have about myself that might be limiting my ability to grow?

2. Where did these beliefs come from and are they valid based on what we have learned in this chapter?

_____

_____

_____

_____

_____

_____

_____

_____

CHAPTER 2:
How Our Minds Learn

● ●

How Does the Brain Learn?

Hopefully you are now convinced that the capacity of your brain is, as Sir John Eccles put it in the last chapter, "endless." With that settled, we can now turn our attention to just how our brain learns and remembers and grows, physiologically.

To illustrate, a number of years ago I was sitting in the gymnasium of my old high school at my 40-year class reunion. I distinctly remember the feeling when I saw Mickey, my dear friend from 40 years ago, walking up the stairs of the bleachers of the opposite side of the gym. Now remember, I had not seen him for 40 years. Yet somehow my brain picked him out of a vast crowd in the gym. I jumped up and yelled "Mickey!" at the top of my lungs. He turned around and recognized me also! This was after 40 years of not seeing each other. Had we changed? You bet! He had gained forty pounds. Whatever hair I had when I was in high school had left decades ago. We were both wearing clothes that we had never seen each other in. He had a different hair style. I had *no* hair. And yet, we recognized each other from 50 feet away.

Now clearly, that recognition could not have stemmed from a simple logical process. I did not rely on checking on his girth and then mentally extrapolate backwards. I did not mentally calculate his height in inches, or use a color comparison guide to determine the color of his skin and hair. My brain simply *knew* him, because he was in, and here's a new term, my "long-term memory. "[19]

How did the brain do it? How did it make Mickey a part of that memory so effectively that I can recall his appearance instantly 40 years later?

Why Do I Need to Understand This?

By understanding this, you will be able to not only understand how the brain records and remembers facts and figures, but more importantly, how it remembers *what I say to myself about myself*. In other words, (and this would be scary if I simply left you here) the brain records everything you say to it about yourself as readily as it records what it sees when it looks at a picture.

The Brain as a Pattern-Detecting Device

Of everything I have ever studied and learned about the workings of the brain, this next statement is one of the most important to understand:

> *The brain is an amazingly subtle and sensitive **pattern-detecting apparatus**. It detects, constructs, and elaborates patterns as a basic, built-in, natural function. It does not have to be taught or motivated to do so, any more than the heart needs to be instructed or coaxed to pump blood.*[20]

So how does the brain do this? You will want to remember this information forever, because it will have a significant affect on your success as a person who is growing, and a life-long learner. When we look at something, our eyes do not recognize it. That is not their job. Their job is simply to perceive light bouncing off of objects. That light is then sent to the brain, and the brain must then go to work. But what does it do…exactly?

If I were to display before you a coffee pot, or a paint brush, you would instantly recognize them effortlessly. However, you were not *born* knowing what these objects are. You *learned* what they were sometime between your birth and the present. All *learning* has taken place in the same way.[21]

This ability that even infants have to gradually sort out an extremely complex, changing world is aptly called, "Making sense of the world."[22] Let's look at one isolated illustration to understand the steps it takes to do so.

It is Only an Image

We raised our two daughters in Rohnert Park, a little enclave 50 miles north of San Francisco. As a result, when they were young, my daughters had no clear concept of what was meant by the word *city*. Figure 1 illustrates what their brains knew about the 'city.' Absolutely nothing. They started with a clean slate.

If my wife or I tell them that a city is a place where many people live close together, they may fail to see why Rohnert Park is not a city. If they visit San Francisco, they will be impressed by the Golden Gate Bridge, traffic noise, the tall buildings, and all the stores. A trip to the shopping center may also impress them as being a city, since they experience crowded sidewalks, many stores, and our multiplex theatre. Yet Rohnert Park is definitely not a city.

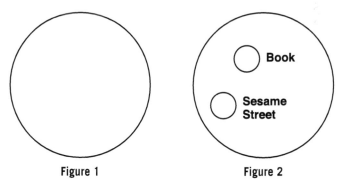

Figure 1   Figure 2

To clarify their concept of the 'city,' let's imagine that I sit with our daughters when they are six and three and read them a book about the city. When I do, their brain records this reading (because it records *everything*—more on that later) as an 'image.' If they watch *Sesame Street*, the brain records another image, as illustrated in Figure 2.

Now if that is all I do because I have erroneously decided that a book and *Sesame Street* should be sufficient to learn about the city, the brain will keep these images for awhile, but over time they will become more and more fuzzy, and they will not become a part of my daughters' long-term memory. In other words, they will not be *learned*. As a result, if I ask them to explain a *city* after I read the book to them, or we watch *Sesame Street* together, they will be able to explain very little.

From an Image to a Pattern

However, in addition to the book and Sesame Street, let's imagine that we provide them with many other experiences regarding a city. All of these experiences provide input. Leslie Hart gives some excellent examples:[23]

- As we drive to a circus, we look at a road map before and they notice "City Limits" for the first time. They see that a city has boundaries.
- They hear a news broadcast that the city population has fallen, and exact figures are given. They have never had a clear idea of what a 'population' meant, but they get the hint that a city has a lot of people.
- A family friend works for the Santa Rosa Fire Department, and another works for the San Francisco Fire Department. So cities might have fire departments.
- They watch a documentary on skyscrapers, so they learn that a city might have very large buildings.
- They visit a Chinese restaurant in San Francisco's China Town, and see that a city has smells, along with street lights and a lot of noise.

All of these images are recorded in your brain as shown in Figure 3.

At this point, the images in Figure 3 are just images. They are simply recorded in their memory (and we are not yet quite sure how that happens...we think it involves a chemical change in the brain). They were input into my daughters' brains randomly through my reading a book to them, going to San Francisco, or watching *Sesame Street*. They are recorded in the same way.

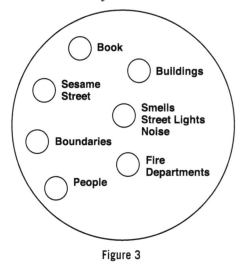

Figure 3

Now the extraction begins.

Here Comes the Trillions of Connections

In time, the brain begins to see relationships among the images. There were buildings in the image of a book, just as there were buildings in the image of *Sesame Street*. It therefore lays down an actual **connection** (called **neural connections**) involving axons, dendrites, and synapses—the components of a neuron—between the image of a book and the image of *Sesame Street*. When it remembers a fire department on *Sesame Street* and a fire department in San Francisco, it creates another neural connection with another set of neurons. It remembers a lot of people in the book, and also a lot of people in *Sesame Street*. It lays down a third neural connection. And on and on. As we learned in the last chapter, the research has discovered that these neural connections, shown in Figure 4, run into the trillions! They also involve many changes in the brain cells themselves. The cells produce more electrochemical energy, form these new connections, remodel nerve endings, improve receptor networks, and revitalize your overall brain function.[24]

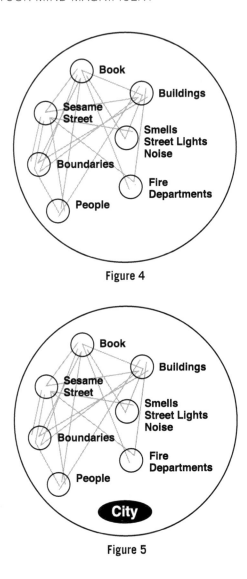

Figure 4

Figure 5

Over time, these neural connections among all of these images form what is called a *pattern* as shown in Figure 5. And the
longer our daughters live and grow, the more this pattern of a
city will sharpen and deepen because of the increasing number
of connections that the brain will create among all of the images
of a city. This pattern of a *city* is now in their longterm memory,
and will be there for as long as they live!

The PFI Process

This process of extracting patterns from images is called the PFI Process (for "Patterns From Images"). It not only summarizes *how we learn*, it leads to our having an unlimited collection of patterns *which we will never lose*! Once a pattern has been set, it is now part of your long-term memory. That is how I remembered Mickey so well from across the gym.

The PFI process is *very* observable in small children. When beginning to talk, a child may point to any man who comes into sight and exclaim, "Daddy!" because she was using *daddy* in the sense of *man*. A little later, guided by such feedback as "No, that is not daddy—daddy is at work," the child would point to men who only came into our house, whether an uncle, or my father, as *daddy*. With further feedback, patterns got straightened out, and becomes a word that only meant the child's father. It takes longer for children to become clear on the fact that their friends also have a daddy, and some years to grasp the relationships; and still more to be able to categorize from people to males, to relatives and friends, neighbors, policeman, mailman, as well as boys, girls and many subtle relationships.

This is a process of learning that Frank Smith and others have aptly called, "Making sense of the world."[25] This "making sense" has also been widely expressed by brain researchers. Harry J. Jerison,[26] for example, suggests that reality is a "creation of the brain, a model of a possible world that makes sense of the mass of information that reaches us through our various sensory systems."

This ability we have to gradually sort out an extremely complex changing world must be considered astounding. But more surprising is the clear fact that we manage to learn from input presented *in a completely random, fortuitous fashion*—unplanned, accidental, unordered, and uncontrolled.[27] The reason for this is embarrassingly simple: The world in which the brain must learn is itself "unplanned, accidental, unordered, and uncontrolled!"

A Summary of the PFI Process

The significance of how we learn by extracting patterns from images carries with it four significant points:

1. **Remember this PFI Methodology Because it Provides the Understanding of What Your Brain Does With Your Self-talk!**

   Enough said—we'll talk about this A LOT in subsequent chapters.

2. **You No Longer Need to Feel Bad About How You Learn**

   If you feel bad because you seem to learn more in a random, chaotic way, you no longer need to. The extraction from patterns in real life is from confusion...because let's face it; life can be confusing! Our brain learns to cope with this...it almost seems to thrive in it at times.

3. **Comparing Yourself to Others Is No Longer Realistic**

   This learning process out of chaos goes on incessantly in each individual in a purely individual way. We all learn differently, because we all have our own chaotic world with which to cope. It is for this reason that comparing yourself to others is not only silly, but unrealistic. My world is incredibly different from yours!

4. **Nothing You Are Learning is Wasted**

   The brain is by nature a magnificent pattern-detecting apparatus. The time it takes for this pattern detection and identification to take place is directly related to how many images, clues, pictures, readings, trips, tables, figures, books, papers, presentations, slides, magazines, and all of the other materials a student is exposed to when a student is learning.

What does this mean to you? That virtually all of what you learn in life is extracted by the brain to be put into patterns.[28] It is for this reason that *nothing* is wasted, even that time when you were out of work, or that divorce, events in your life that may seem meaningless to you, or even tragic! The more images, clues, and reading you can expose yourself to, the more you will learn and grow. In other words, the more you learn about a subject, and the more ways you learn, the more intelligent you are about that particular subject.

I heard of a man who had a number of tragedies happen in his life, including his wife and daughter dying at a relatively young age. He told his pastor, who was at his bedside just before he passed away after a very long terminal illness, "I would never have chosen many of the things that happened during my life. But, I would *not trade* them for the world!"

Next Chapter Preview

Now that we understand how any mind learns, in the next chapter we will delve into how *you* learn.

Remnants to Remember

1. The brain is an amazingly sensitive pattern-detecting apparatus that detects, constructs, and elaborates patterns as a basic, built-in, natural function. It does not have to be taught or motivated to do so, any more than the heart needs to be instructed or coaxed to pump blood.

2. Thinking is really a process of "Making sense of the world." It is your brain's attempt to make sense of the mass of information that reaches you throughout the day through what you hear, smell, taste, touch, and feel.

3. Learning takes place in this chaotic world incessantly and in each individual in a purely individual way. We all learn differently, so comparing ourselves to others is not only silly, but unrealistic. My world is incredibly different from yours!

A Point to Ponder

"Nothing you are learning is wasted." Why do you think this is true?

_____

_____

_____

_____

_____

_____

_____

_____

_____

_____

CHAPTER THREE:
How *Your* Mind Learns

• •

So How Does *My* Brain Learn?

In the last chapter, we learned that your brain extracts patterns from information and images you are learning. Since my background is with college students, let's use them as an example by imagining that *you* are one of my new students taking Human Anatomy for the first time. Figure 1 represents what you know right now about Human Anatomy: Absolutely nothing.

After a couple of classes, you begin to lay down images for each of the terms you have learned, as shown in Figure 2.

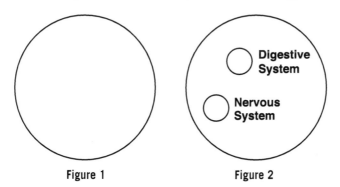

Figure 1   Figure 2

It is important to note that at this point, the images are figuratively floating around your brain, because your brain has not yet had the time to perceive any relationships between them. Over time, however, the brain does lay down more images, discerns relationships, and lays down neural connections, as shown in Figure 3.

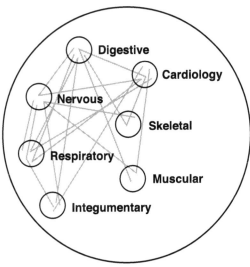

Figure 3

As you learn more and the brain records more and more images, it then begins to also extract patterns for each of the systems you are learning: Digestive, nervous, respiratory, etc. Just as the concept of a city sharpened in our daughters, these new patterns also sharpen and deepen, based on the increasing number of connections that the brain creates from these images. Again…this is the *process of learning,* and it leads to our possessing a vast collection of patterns that runs into the millions and neural connections that run into the trillions!

An Example of the PFI Process

Read the following paragraph:

> I cdnuolt blveiee taht I cluod aulaclty uesdnatnrd waht I was rdanieg. Aoccdrnig to rscheearch at Cmabrigde Uinervtisy, it deosn't mttaer in waht oredr the ltteers in a wrod are, the olny iprmoatnt tihng is taht the frist and lsat ltteer be in the rghit pclae. The rset can be a taotl mses and you can sitll raed it wouthit a porbelm. Tihs is bcuseae the huamn mnid deos not raed ervey lteter by istlef, but the wrod as a pttaern. Amzanig huh? yaeh and I awlyas tghuhot slpeling was ipmorantt!

Why can you read the preceding paragraph? Your brain has created a pattern for every word you know, and now it instantly recognizes each pattern by simply seeing the *first and last letter* of each word. Since every word you use is a pattern, you can only imagine how many trillions of patterns your brain is carrying around.

Applying What We Have Learned

The significance of how you learn by extracting patterns from images carries with it three significant concepts:

1. Learning Takes Time

This pattern-detecting process doesn't happen overnight; it takes time. By the end of the first week in my medical terminology course, I could always sense a great deal of fear in many of my new students. Most often, I would hear something like: "I am too old for this!" or "I have been out of school too long!"

Why did learning seem to be "not happening"? Their brains, which had only had a few days to record the new images, *had not yet made the connections between the images.* In other words, without these connections, the images are figuratively floating around their minds (as shown in Figure 4) without any real understanding as to where they belong, or how they are related to the other images. This creates a lot of fear and frustration.

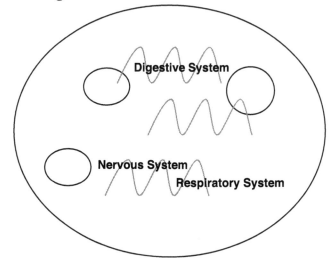

Figure 4

2. Be Careful of Listening to What Your Brain is Saying

At this point of fear and confusion, the brain usually resorts to lies, such as, "I am so dumb!" or "I am so slow!" We will learn why our brains do this in subsequent chapters. However, these lies could not be further from the truth. The new students' brains are simply trying to make sense out of what they have been given. However, the search for neural connections and relationships does not happen overnight. It takes time, and because it takes time, we sometimes become very impatient, and feel "slow" or "dim" or "thick."

What can you do with these feelings? Primarily, realize that there is no concept, no fact of brain-based learning, more directly important than this:

> *The brain detects, constructs, and elaborates patterns as a basic, built-in, natural function. It does not have to be taught or motivated to do so, any more than our heart needs to be instructed or coaxed to pump blood. In fact, efforts to teach or motivate the detection of patterns, however well meaning, can often have inhibiting and negative effects.*[29]

In other words, most of your fear comes from wanting your brain to learn and grow faster. You need to realize, however, that the brain has been creating patterns and connecting information since the dawn of mankind, and it doesn't like to rush. In fact, if we attempt to rush the brain, the neural connections that *are* made will not be clear and may not "stick." Hence, "cramming" before a test may help the student feel somewhat prepared, but after the test the information is figuratively floating again, and (usually) inaccessible.

3. We All Learn Differently

A third key point to remember regarding how you learn is this: Although all of us learn through this process, the extractions and patterns are unique to each one of us. The reason is that we have a First Nature and a Second Nature. Our First Nature is what we were born with...our natural disposition, we temperament, and character. It is established by the time we are three to five years old.

Everything else is Second Nature, and is composed of everything you have learned and are learning now. Learning new information is a continuous process, and it comes from our parents, caregivers, siblings, reading, TV, movies, friends, school, church, job, trips, vacations …and on and on and on.

Thus, our Second Nature is quite unique to us. In fact, much of our learning lies in that uniqueness. This fact not only makes what we have learned totally ours, but a permanent part of our memory, and ultimately who we have become, and are still becoming. It is not only the reason I recognized Mickey from across the basketball court, it is also the reason I was who I was 40 years ago, and who I am today.

We Build on What We Already Know

When it can, our brains create patterns from patterns that are already there![30] In other words, the PFI process is heavily based upon our past experience; on what we have already learned. Let's use an example. When one of my students has just completed the first week of college, he often feels overwhelmed. Usually I hear a protest such as, "I am too old for this!" I respond exactly the opposite of what he expects. I congratulate him, and we talk about the significant advantage his age gives to his educational experience. He has this advantage because he has far more life experiences than my younger students, and although it may take a bit longer, his brain will soon learn new information more completely.

All of these principles will be running like a thread through this text.

Next Chapter Preview

We have learned that your brain is the most amazing and complex structure in the known universe. Its capacity to learn and grow however is limited by one predominant factor: How much *you* see yourself learning and growing and changing. The next chapter then will begin to explore the fact that almost all permanent change must begin with how you think—not what you are doing. More specifically, the changes must begin with how you see yourself.

Remnants to Remember

1. Learning usually takes time and does not happen overnight.
2. Be careful about listening to your brain's thoughts. When your brain whispers little innuendos such as, "I am too old" or "I am too slow," it could usually not be further from the truth. It is simply trying to make sense out of what it has been given, and when it does *not* make sense, it becomes very defensive. However, because learning can at times take so much time, it sometimes becomes very impatient. When this happens, it often feels "slow" or "dim" or "thick."
3. We all learn differently, so never compare how you learn with someone else.
4. In large part, how we learn is based on what we already know.

Points to Ponder

1. Think back on an experience: A sound, smell or touch, that brings back a memory that you had not thought about for a long time. Now, describe it:

```
_____

_____

_____

_____

_____

_____

_____
```

2. All of us seem to have automatic thoughts that keep cropping up in our heads that keep us from learning new things. List just one of those thoughts. How could you change that thought to allow learning to take place?

```
_____

_____

_____

_____

_____

_____

_____
```

CHAPTER FOUR:

Why Is My Self-Image So Important?

● ●

A Brief Review

We've established that the brain is the most amazing and complex structure in the known universe. In fact, as we shall learn in this chapter, its capacity for learning and growth and change is only limited by how much *you* really want to learn and grow and change.

You really *do* want to change. That's why you're reading this book. However, we will see over and over that change must begin on the inside, not on the outside. That is why New Year's resolutions do not work: Because you are concentrating on what you are doing, rather than how you are thinking. More specifically, *change must begin with how you see yourself.*

Joy Bauer expresses this so well in her book *Joy's Life Diet* when she says, "All of the successful dieters I've worked with say that they had to know in their hearts that they would succeed this time. Success starts in the head, moves to the heart, and lastly involves the heart and stomach."[31]

How you see yourself is called your *self-image*. You have thousands of them. They are stored in your subconscious mind, so let's learn about that next.

The Conscious and the Subconscious[a] Mind

A lot more goes on in our minds than what we see, hear, taste, touch, and feel. In fact, most mental activity takes place *out of* the conscience realm. It's for that reason that the whole sphere of unconscious activity is placed under a psychological umbrella called either the "unconscious" or "subconscious."

The Subconscious Mind

The conscious mind is easiest to understand because we are aware of it all day long. One of its functions is called perception through your senses—sight, taste, touch, smell, and hearing. However, you store this information on the *subconscious* level, not the conscious. In fact, while you were in your mother's womb, you started recording information on the subconscious level.[32] (Actually, every experience you've ever had is recorded in the subconscious.)

I find this fascinating: We do NOT record the actual event, but *our* version of the event, and then we call it the "truth"—not "our" truth, but "the" truth. We think that what we experience must be the way life really is. You say, "I see the way life really is!" And I say "No...*I* see the way life really is!"

We're *both* wrong; and this dichotomy will form the first of a list of Brain Principles that appears throughout this book. This first one is one of the most important!

Brain Principle One

We behave and act not according to the truth, but the truth as we *believe* it to be!

Let's me say it again: **We behave and act not according to the truth, but the truth as we *believe* it to be!**

---

[a]The term subconscious was coined by psychologist Pierre Janet (1849–1947), who credited it with a hidden level of awareness and automatism. The term also appears in Sigmund Freud's very early work. Although the use of the term "subconscious" is now largely avoided in academic settings, it remains popular in common use. Since "unconscious" and "subconscious" are synonymous, I will be using the term "subconscious" throughout this text.

To illustrate my point, let's start with some optical illusions I have used in my classes, followed by a true story that sheds light on this point even more clearly.

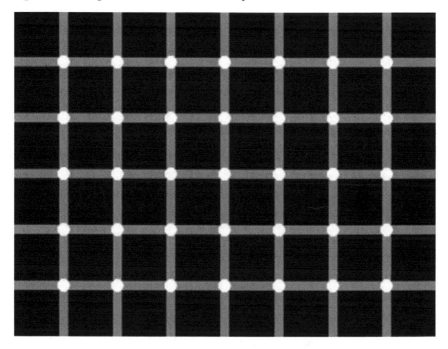

Count the black dots

Are the horizontal lines parallel or do they slope?

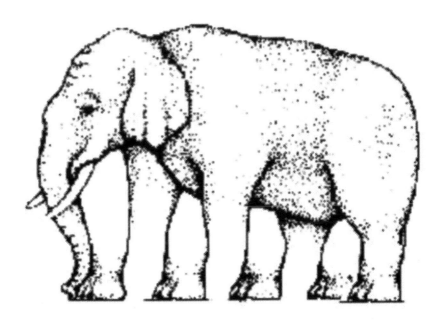

How many legs does this elephant have?

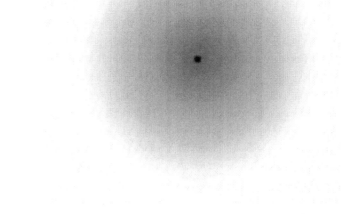

Keep staring at the black dot. After a while the gray haze around it will appear to shrink.

Is the book coming toward you... or away from you?

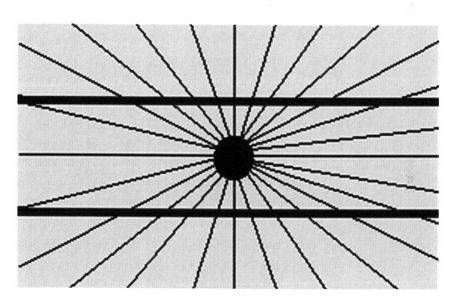

Are the thicker horizontal lines straight or bent?

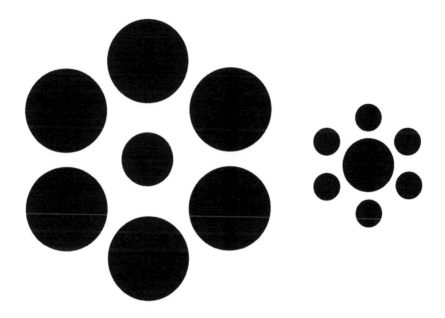

Which circle in the middle is bigger?

Is this possible?

All of these are really fun (in fact, I suggest that you try them on your friends!). These optical illusions illustrate the fact that what we see is not always as "truthful" as we would like. But how does this apply to the subconscious?

Believe me...the next story does! It vividly illustrates the principle that we truly do **behave and act not according to the truth, but the truth as we *believe* it to be**!

The Story of Cliff Young

If you Google "Cliff Young" on the Internet, you will find him on a lot of Web sites, including Wikipedia, and another titled, "Cliff Young, a farmer who inspired a nation."[33]

In 1983 when Cliff was 61 years old, he entered a marathon in Australia that stretched from Sydney to Melbourne, a distance of some 875 kilometers (543 miles). More than 150 world-class athletes showed up, all the so-called "best in the world" at marathon running. Among this group of world-class runners, it was surprising to see this character named Cliff Young appear on the day of the race, especially because he was wearing overalls and galoshes over his work boots (called "muck boots). His only trainer? His 81-year-old mother.

Naturally, reporters crowded around to interview this elderly potato farmer with no teeth. When they asked why he was there, he answered this way: "I grew up on a farm where we couldn't afford horses, and the whole time I was growing up until about four years ago, whenever the storms would roll in, I'd have to go out and round up the sheep. We had 2,000 head, and we have 2,000 acres. Sometimes I would have to run those sheep for two or three days. It took a long time, but I'd catch them. I believe I can run this race; it's only two more days. Five days. I've run sheep for three."

The race began, and guess what? Not only did Cliff Young win the race, he beat the best runners in the world by a day and a half!

How? Well, if you are world-class runner, you know the "truth", which is that you run for 18 hours and sleep six. But Cliff did not know the "truth." He did not know that you were supposed to...sleep. So while the rest of the runners were sleeping, he just kept running.

After being awarded the first prize of $10,000, Cliff said he didn't know there was a prize, and insisted that he had not entered for the money. He said, "There are five other runners still out there doing it tougher than me," and he gave them each $2,000. He did not keep a single cent for himself. That act endeared him to all of Australia. Cliff, a humble, average man, undertook an extraordinary feat and became a national sensation.

If I ended Cliff's story now, it would be very "inspirational!" But... I am NOT writing this to 'inspire' you; for both you and I know that 'inspiration' lasts about three days, and then we go back to the way we were before. No... I am writing this to help us change the way we think! So let's look at what happened the following year.

Cliff entered the race the following year but injured himself to the point where he could not finish. However, many of the other runners, now knowing a "new truth," no longer slept... and beat his record. And the year after that... and the year after that! Now, almost nobody sleeps during the Australian Marathon.

The "truth" now is that to win that race, you must run like Cliff Young, using a running technique coined the "Young Shuffle" where you do not pick up your feet as marathoners have always done. Studies have since determined that this technique is far more aerodynamic and expends less energy.

You also must run all night as well as all day.

Where does this lead us? Simply this (and please, remember this for the rest of your life, because it will significantly affect how you live your life): **We behave and act *not according to the truth*, but the truth as we believe it to be**. This "truth" is based on how we see ourselves, just as Cliff Young based his running on how he saw himself. This "truth" about ourselves is wrapped up in our self-image, of which we have thousands, all stored in our subconscious. (We will explore our self-image in detail in the next chapter.) In turn, our behavior is based on those self-images. If the "truth" about ourselves is therefore less than our actual potential...what we can really do...or become...or grow into...we behave accordingly. In fact, we will discover in the next chapter that it's the brain's job to make sure that what you do is based on how you see yourself—your self-image.

Next Chapter Preview

We will learn in the next chapter that if you say, "No Way!" the brain must *block out the way*. On the other hand, if you say, "Absolutely. Of course I can do that!" the brain will *find a way*. Henry Ford said it so well: "Whether you think that you can, or that you can't, you are usually right."[34]

Now, all of this can be truly enlightening, even inspirational. However, **inspiration does *not* produce change!** At some time in your life you have no doubt been tremendously inspired by someone you heard, or something you read, and you said to yourself, **This time...from now on...I will do such and such** or **Stop doing so and so**. And you may even change...*for a while.* And then you usually return to the same pattern...sometimes sooner, or sometimes later. WHY IS THIS? We'll find out in the next chapter!

Remnants to Remember

Brain Principle One: We behave and act not according to the truth, but the truth as we *believe* it to be!

⁇ Points to Ponder

1. What are beliefs I have about myself?

_____
_____
_____
_____
_____
_____
_____
_____
_____

2. How were these beliefs about myself formed?

_____
_____
_____
_____
_____
_____
_____
_____
_____

3. What are some "truths" in my life that are probably not really truthful?

_____

_____

_____

_____

_____

_____

_____

_____

CHAPTER FIVE:

A Second Look at Your Self-image

• •

Let's Review What We Have Learned So Far

After discovering how amazing our mind is, we saw that if we want change in our lives, we must *begin* with the mind—and specifically with how we see ourselves (called our self-image). We also looked at Brain Principle One: **We behave and act *not according to the truth*, but the truth as we believe (or perceive) it to be**.

We saw that the "truth" for Cliff Young was that you run without sleeping. Initially, this contradicted the "truth" of 150 world-class runners...until Cliff beat them by a day and a half. Now, their "new truth" is that you do not sleep when you run the Sydney to Melbourne Marathon.

We then saw that this "truth" is wrapped up in our self-image, of which we have thousands, all stored in our subconscious. We also learned that our behavior is based on our self-image, so if our self-image is less than our actual potential...what we can really do...or become...or grow into...we behave accordingly. In this chapter we discover why this is. We will also begin to talk about how to change this. Before we do, however, we need to look at **Brain Principle Two**.

Brain Principle Two:

The brain is a literal mechanism that accepts what you tell it without argument.

In other words, when you say "I can't do it!" your brain says, "OK You can't." When you have a huge yawn and exclaim how tired you are, the brain says, "OK I didn't know that, but I'll make sure you feel that way." On the other hand, when you exclaim, "I thought this was hard, but it is so easy!" The brain agrees, and actually MAKES IT EASY FOR YOU!

Remember this forever, for it will make a significant difference in the way you run your life. In fact, the rest of this chapter is based on this principle.

The Job of the Creative Subconscious

In the last chapter, we learned that your *conscious* mind perceives information through your senses—hearing, smelling, touching, tasting, and seeing. It is responsible for your *perception*. Your *subconscious* then stores all this information and calls it the "truth." We saw, however, that we store our own version of the "truth," and that this version is different for each of us. My version of the truth is different from yours, and yours is different from mine. This is what makes life so interesting! Finally, we learned that the subconscious also stores our self-image.

Now I am introducing a new player: The **creative subconscious**. Of its three functions (and we will eventually learn all of them), the first is the most important: Make sure that what you do, and how you think, *lines up with your self-image*.

Let me give you an example. If my "truth" about me is that I see myself as shy, I don't need to remember to act shy. My creative subconscious makes sure that I act shy.

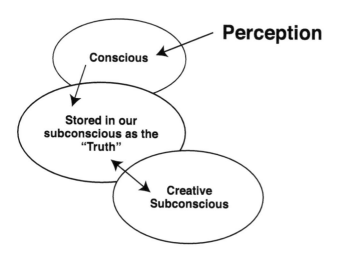

The No.1 job of the Creative Subconscious: Maintain sanity

In other words, its job is to always maintain your idea of "the truth." Another phrase for this is "Maintaining Sanity." Its job is to make you *behave like you think you are*; to make sure you act like your self-image. In other words, once you know who and how you are, the subconscious automatically takes over. It makes you behave like the person you know yourself to be.[35] You never need to think about it. So if you are outgoing and gregarious, you don't have to remember to act outgoing or gregarious. When you know who you are, you don't need get up in the morning and remember to be that way. Your creative subconscious makes sure you behave like you know you are.

The Downside of the Creative Subconscious

There is a downside to this—Your creative subconscious does this without ever asking *if what you think about yourself is true*. It does not care! Its job is to make sure that you **act like you believe you are!** In fact, you have no choice. This alone explains **why change can be so difficult!** In fact, many of the chapters in this book are devoted to how you can change.

True-life stories are the best way to teach this, especially when you have lived it yourself. When my wife, Mary, and I were driving away from my father's memorial service about 30 years ago, she looked at me and said, "If you die early, I'll kill you! I want for us to enjoy our life together growing old."

At the time I was about 30 pounds overweight so I said to myself, "You're right! I really need to lose 30 pounds!"

On the Monday following the memorial service, I got up early and ran for 30 minutes. I did the same on Wednesday, Friday, and Saturday. I also swam on Tuesday and Thursday. I also limited my breakfast to a grapefruit and toast, had carrot juice for lunch, and for dinner had asparagus with a small piece of fish or chicken (and I *hate* asparagus!) By the end of that first week, I had lost about 3 pounds, which is A LOT in one week.

However, come Saturday morning, I would get up, make a pecan pie (or the equivalent)...and eat the whole thing over the weekend. All the weight I had lost during the week was gained back by Monday morning.

I did this off and on for 25 years! However, after learning what I am teaching in this book, I realized that I was giving myself the wrong message. When I said to myself, "I am a 230-pound man who needs to lose 30 pounds," my creative subconscious *made sure* that I ate and exercised like a 230-pound man, *whether it was good for me or not!* That is its job! As I said above, the job of the creative subconscious is to make sure that I act *like I believe I am*, and not what I "should" be, or can be. (Even if it is not good for me...the creative subconscious did not care.)

After studying what I am sharing with you now, I changed my self-talk to, "I love weighing only 200 pounds because it makes me feel great about myself." Over time, I found myself eating and exercising like a 200-pound man. Why? Because I had learned how to override the image of a 230-pound man to one who weighed 200 pounds. My creative subconscious then caused me to eat and exercise like a 200-pound man, not a 230-pound man.

That, in a nutshell, is how change comes about. Now...there is far more to changing how we think, and we'll be learning this in subsequent chapters.

Here's another point: The creative subconscious is *continually checking and balancing* your behavior, based on your self-image. I saw this in one of my students named Susie.

Susie's Story

Susie approached me on the first day of my calculus class to inform me that she was a "C" student in math; always had been, always would be. When I told her that I would help her raise that grade, she became very skeptical. "I have *always* been a C student in math, so I doubt there is much you could do, no matter how good a teacher you are."

I worked with Suzie and was therefore not surprised when she received an A on her first test. When she held it in her hand, do you know what she said to me? "Oops! It must be a *mistake!*" I asked her to explain. Susie told me that she had *never* received an A on a math test, and that she must have just been "lucky!" She went on to say that since she had gotten an A, she would not have to study as hard for the next test to maintain her C. "But why not get an A on *every* test?" I pleaded. Her answer: "Because I'm a *C* student."

Sure enough, she flunked the next test and got her C in the course. Why? Because she saw herself as a C student.

So with that first test in hand, I asked Susie, "What would you have done if you had failed this test!? "Oh!" she said. "I would have studied like crazy to get an A on the next one!" "Exactly!" I exclaimed. "So why not just get an A on every test! "Oh, I can't!" she said! "I'm a C student in Math, and C students don't get A's on their Math tests!"

Elementary school principals have learned that when they deal with extremely disruptive and troubled students, they *cannot* complement them when their behavior significantly improves. The reason? The students will usually return to the old behavior. Their creative subconscious is simply making sure that their behavior lines up with their disruptive and troubled self-image.

Can You See How Much We Limit Ourselves

One of the best stories I have ever heard comes from a section in Lou Tice's book *Thought Patterns for a Successful Career* which I am quoting here.[36]

> "*We had adopted some children and among them were three boys. When they were five, six and seven, they were taken away from their mother and fathers, whoever the fathers were. They were badly abused; were beat up, run over, and shot at. Their impression of the world, by the time we got them, was the world beats me up and I'm not a good person—because it had. Now, we were going to be the best mother and father anybody could be. We didn't know much about this stuff in those days, so every time those kids did something good, we'd tell them, "Nice going." The nicer we were to them, the worse they behaved.*

> "*When you know you're not a good person and the world out here is treating you differently than you know you are, you must subconsciously make the people "out there" treat you like you know you are. The first day my six-year-old went to kindergarten, or the first grade, the sheriff brought him home arrested. And then things got worse. It wasn't going to get better. When we would complement them on something that went well, they'd start a fire behind the couch or in the closet. I'd take the kid, slam him in a chair, and say, "What did you start the fire for?" Guess what he said? "I don't know." "What do you mean you don't know? You just started the fire! Now get in your room till you can figure it out." See, he was setting us up to punish him. We were treating him nice, but it was so different from the way he knew his world to be, that his behavior—not consciously, but subconsciously—to make you or me act toward him like he knows the world.*"

Mr. Tice's children reflect the observations of Robert K. Cooper, Ph. D. in his wonderful book *Get Out of Your Own Way*. He observes that millions of people get thin(ner) and then gain back all of the weight and more. Others become the number one performer and then, trophy in hand, begin to decline.[37] In addition, an alarming percentage of lottery winners lose all the money they have won.[38]

Why? Because the creative subconscious in each of Mr. Tice's children does not see themselves as loved, or Mr. Cooper's people as thin, or the lottery winners as rich. So its job is to make sure that it undercuts that love, gains that weight back, and loses that money!

This is why when, having lost your keys, you could be looking right at them without ever seeing them. Finally, someone else shows you that they were in front of you the entire time. "If they were any closer they would have bit ya!" Why didn't you see them? Because when you tell yourself, "I have lost my keys," your brain said, "OK!" and makes sure you don't see them.

Isn't that amazing?

This phenomenon is an example of the famous principle of Norbert Wiener, the founding father of the computer. He coined the phrase *GIGO*, which simply means Garbage In, Garbage Out. We accept so much garbage in our lives—criticism from other people, or we tell ourselves that we cannot do something, or we are too fat, or too thin, or not attractive, or horrible at math. We need to realize that our subconscious accepts that garbage without question! Again, our mind is a literal mechanism! It doesn't stop there. The creative subconscious not only accepts the garbage, it then ACTS upon that garbage as if it were true. So, we gain the weight back, we undermine our relationships, and we throw away our money.

Next Chapter Preview

Since changing ourselves involves changing our self-images, we will learn where they come from in the next chapter.

Remnants to Remember

1. **Brain Principle Two: The brain is a literal mechanism that accepts what you tell it without argument.**

2. In other words, we behave like the person we think we are. Another way of saying it is that we behave as we see ourselves.

3. The wonderful news, however, is that we now know this. The brain is no longer a mysterious "black box." Cognitive psychology has discovered these wonderful principles in just the last 40 years of research, and they are discovering more all the time! We also know that we can change our thinking, and how we see ourselves and, as a result, how we live!

 # Point to Ponder

1. What examples of the Garbage In/Garbage Out principle have affected how you see yourself?

_____
_____
_____
_____
_____
_____
_____
_____
_____

CHAPTER SIX:

Where Does Our Self-Image Come From?

● ●

"For as a man thinkest in his heart, so is he"
Proverbs 23:7

A Review of What We Have Learned

We have learned that the process of learning and changing and growing must begin on the inside...with our magnificent mind. However, we learned through the optical illusions in Chapter Four that our brain does not consistently see things accurately. In fact, our brain is lightning quick at jumping to conclusions, and is often wrong.[39] Based on this fact, we learned our First Brain Principle: **We behave and act *not according to the truth*, but the truth as we (i.e., our mind) *believe* (or perceive) it to be**. We saw an excellent example of this through 61 year-old Cliff Young, whose truth was that you don't sleep when you run a marathon in Australia.

We also have learned that this "truth" is wrapped up in our thousands of self-images. These self-images determine what we believe and feel about ourselves. They are in turn based on what we tell them through our self-talk. These facts led to Brain Principle Two, which simply states that **The brain is a literal mechanism that accepts what you tell it without argument**.

This is equivalent to Norbert Weiner's Garbage-in, Garbage-out principle. When we accept statements about ourselves—whether they are true or not—the brain also accepts them as true…and it acts upon them as if they *were* true.

So Where Does our Self-Image Come From?

Why are some of us born feeling naturally great about ourselves, and others not so great, depending upon our family, our culture, our wealth or poverty? This whole subject touches the "Nature vs. Nurture" controversy that has been raging for centuries (and will not be resolved in a 230-page book). Briefly, the controversy pits the influence that our genes (i.e., our "nature") have on how we learn, versus how we learn by simply living our lives ("our nurturing").

Suffice it to say that such traits as your physical appearance and your temperament were acquired from your genes. **But as we shall learn in this chapter,** *everything* **else is learned, including your self-image**. You were not born feeling great about yourself…or bad about yourself. That was all learned.

Before we learn how, let's remember that we do not have one self-image, but thousands. How I see myself as an athlete, as a teacher, as a husband, as a cook, as a skier are all self-images, and all of them have been learned. We will concentrate on how one was learned, and then extract some principles from how it happened.

I was raised with sisters: Two older and one younger, and it is commonly known that girls mature more rapidly than boys. My sisters were no exception, and they seemed to excel at everything. They were, and are, very smart. The oldest was always the first to raise her hand in class, the next was always consumed by some wonderful passion, and my youngest sister seemed to always have a heart of gold. And ALL of them got A's in all their classes.

I, however, did not get A's. My mind didn't care much for school; I was easily distracted by imaginary worlds I would often create while sitting at my desk. I loved drawing pictures of roller coasters on a piece of paper, and then use my pencil to imagine myself in the coaster swirling around the hairpin turns on the paper. As a result, subjects like math held no interest to me. In fact, I don't think I passed math once in elementary school. At the end of every school year, just before the report cards were handed out I would be shaking because I was so afraid of being held back. My father, who loved me very much, and who was a very patient man, could not understand how his daughters did so well in school, while his only son had F's in math on every report card.

Our family was right out of the 1950s, scripted out of the television programs *Father Knows Best* and *The Donna Reed Show*. Dinner was promptly served at 5:30, Grace was said, and everyone would discuss their day. While I listened and talked, I was also making magnificent castles with my mashed potatoes (and hiding the brussel sprouts in my pocket, to be discarded later). At the end of dinner, my father would slowly push himself away from the table, look at me rather somberly, rise to his full six-foot height, and say in his deepest voice, "All right, Steven, let's go do your math."

Now what was really happening here? Research has discovered that we communicate through what we actually say, our tone of voice, and our body language. What we say accounts for about 10 percent of the overall message; our body language comprises 50 percent; and our tone makes up the remaining 40 percent.[40] In other words, more than 90 percent of our communication is nonverbal. And the nonverbal signals which my father was displaying were communicating very clearly his frustration over trying to teach me math.

What did my self-talk say? "You cannot understand math!"

Can you guess what would happen? As soon as my father began his tutoring, my brain would go blank. Why? Because my self-talk was telling me that I could not do math, so why even try? After all, my father was the grownup, the authority, the father who thought (although he never did) that his son would never understand math. My self-talk therefore told me the same thing.

The frustration that my teachers exhibited only added to this, along with my failing math tests, my F's on my incompleted homework, and the F's on all the report cards. In addition, I myself then *added to my* own self-talk (we ALL do this) by saying that I must not be very smart. "If I can't understand math, I won't be able to understand anything else!" And what did my brain do! It agreed! "OK" it said, "If you say so! You're not very smart!" As we have discovered, that is the job of the creative subconscious!

Do you remember in Chapter Two where we learned how our mind learns? Our daughters, Abigail and Sarah, learned about the city through books and pictures and trips and all of the other images, which were added and connected together to form a pattern of a city, as shown in Figure 1.

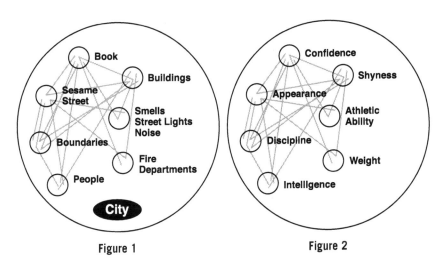

Figure 1   Figure 2

Our self-image is learned the same way, as shown in Figure 2!

Just as my self-image about my ability to learn math was based on what other people told me, and what I told myself, and the F's on my math tests, and F's on the report cards, and homework, all of our self-images are built the same way. Here's the scary part: This image I had of myself as not being very smart lasted for 35 years. But years later, when I was 42, I found myself teaching in a college, and do you know what my favorite subject was? You guessed it. Math! Why? As soon as new college students hear university math is in their curriculum, they look like a deer caught in headlights. Their fear is almost palpable. I knew *exactly* what they were feeling—because I had felt the same way myself.

As a result, I became obsessed with understanding how the brain works and learns, and began developing ways of teaching math that were unthreatening, fun, and actually worked! My students began loving and learning math. In fact, math became their favorite subject. This all came from me, the one who "was never very smart." I ended up writing two college textbooks on computer software and—you guessed it—math.

What happened? Did I suddenly become smart in math when I reached my midforties? Obviously not! Let's examine what happened by adding some additional Brain Principles to our list.

Brain Principle Three

Our self-image is based on our self-talk.
Although we will explore the depths of self-talk in Chapter 12, let's define it here. Your self-talk is simply that conversation you are having with yourself all day long. And A LOT is being said. In fact, when someone is talking to you, you are talking to yourself three times faster. When they stop talking, it increases six times faster.

Not only is this persistent chatter going on, your brain is recording *everything* you are saying, whether it is true or not, or good for you or not. No questions asked. This corresponds with Brain Principle Two that we learned in the last chapter: **The brain is a literal mechanism that accepts what you tell it without argument**. Everything you tell yourself about your-self, whether positive or negative, whether true or untrue, is ac-cepted by your self-image as absolutely true. Your brain simply records what you tell it.[41] This is why I had trouble with math; not because I was unintelligent, but because my self-talk told me that I simply could not understand math. My brain accepted what it was told, and it became a part of one of my self-images.

Brain Principle Four

Your brain is not recording what is happening, it is recording your *version* of what is happening.

As I mentioned in Chapter Two, your eyes simply take in light reflecting off objects. Your brain does the work. It records what it thinks you are seeing based on what it has learned in the past. The reason is because your brain is recording your *version* of what you are seeing...or hearing...or smelling. So when my father said in his deep, melodious voice, "All right, Steven, let's go do your math," my version of what my father was saying was, "My father does not believe I can understand math." As I grew older, I discovered that my father had *always* believed that I was smart. My self-talk, however, recorded the opposite, and my self-image then acted on that version.

This also goes back to what we discussed in the last chapter about the creative subconscious *continually checking and balancing* our behavior.

I remember the only time that I ever got an A on a math test in elementary school. Do you know what I said? "Wow! It must be a mistake!" I did not congratulate myself, nor did I study for the next test. After all, if you are an F student in math, you get F's. You guessed it! I flunked the next math test. Why? Because the "truth" in my self-image was that I could not do math.

Brain Principle Five

You must agree with the opinion of another about you before it becomes a part of your self-image.[42]

I stated in Chapter Two that the brain being "an amazing ***pattern-detecting apparatus***" is a statement which is "one of the most important to understand." Brain Principle Five runs a close second. When a professional tutor was hired to take over my tutoring sessions in math, I remember him exclaiming in exasperation one time, "You really *don't* understand this, do you!" My brain recorded his statement as a new "truth" which was then added to the other "truths" in my math self-image. Why?

Well, he was a "professional tutor" so he must know I can't do math.

If I had been 15 years older, I might have responded to him by saying something like, "Who are you to tell me that? I *can* understand math." If I had, his opinion would NOT have become a part of my self-image. But at the age of eight, that was not really an option.

In other words, people might be your greatest critics, or give you their opinions about your abilities or character, but *you must agree with them before their opinions or statements become a part of your self-image.* Lou Tice refers to this as "Giving Sanction."[43]

Suppose someone says unkind things about you behind your back, or snubs you to your face. These are just words. No word or gesture can, in and of itself, hurt you unless you think it can—unless you let it or *make it* hurt.[44]

Changing this is deceptively simple. You must simply become very skeptical regarding what people say to you about you, especially if their opinions don't fit the person that you want to become. (Much more on this later!)

Brain Principle Six

Your *own* self-talk has *as much an affect* on your self-image as what others say to you.

When we do something stupid, we exclaim, "How could I have been so stupid?!" But, we don't stop there! The conversation goes something like this: "How could I have been so stupid?! Well that's easy to answer. Don't you remember what you did last week? Oh, yeah, I remember that! And last year, that was really stupid, too! Plus, you were the slowest reader in the second grade. You remember that, don't you? Oh, yeah—I had almost forgotten!"

I have seen this kind of self-talk can go on in people for hours…some for weeks …months…years…some for their entire lives!

Here is the clincher: The brain records these memories and beliefs *as if they were brand new, as if they had just happened!*

And, those are a lot of memories and beliefs: About 12,000 to 50,000 per day, according to the National Science Foundation, depending upon how deeply you think.[45]

We must therefore learn to be very careful about what we say to ourselves. (More on that later.)

And, finally...

Brain Principle Seven

You can override those self-images with new ones.

However, it is important to understand at this point that you are not reading this book to change your self-image.

Wait a minute! I thought the whole purpose of this book was to change me?

The answer lies in a principle we have already learned, which is that you are not made up of one self-image, but thousands. This simply means that you will be learning how to change *some* of your self-images; the ones you *want* to change. You will also be learning how you can choose which ones you would like to change. Some you like. Others you would love to simply throw out. And others you have wanted to change for a long time. Those are the ones on which we will concentrate.

Will it be easy? For some of them, yes. Others, though, will be more challenging. But when you work diligently with your mental, emotional, and behavioral tools that you will soon be learning, you will truly understand how to make your mind your motivator, to make it magnificent.

Next Chapter Preview

We have learned the job of the creative subconscious is to make sure what we do lines up with our self-images. As you'll recall from Chapter Five, when I saw myself as a 200-pound man, my self-images made sure I ate and exercised like a 200-pound man. However, as we will learn in the next chapter, there are times our self-images must create blind spots to make this happen.

Remnants to Remember

The reason you are reading this book is to change yourself, which is synonymous with changing your self-images, images that are based on your own self-talk, what others have said to you, and how they have reacted to you. We have learned in this chapter that other than those traits which you acquired from your genes, everything else in your life, including your self-images, have been learned, and although they cannot be deleted (except through a frontal-lobotomy), they can be overridden. We will be learning how to do that.

We have also added a number of Brain Principles in this chapter:

1. We behave and act not according to the truth, but the truth as we *believe* it to be!
2. The brain is a literal mechanism that accepts what you tell it without argument.
3. Our self-image is based on our self-talk.
4. Your brain is not recording what is happening, but your *version* of what is happening.
5. You must agree with the opinion of another about you before it becomes a part of your self-image.
6. Your *own* self-talk has *as much an affect* on your self-image as what others say to you.
7. You are not doomed to the same self-images for your entire life. They can be overridden.

Points to Ponder

1. Can I think of some examples where one of my self-images was a reflection of my self-talk?

_____

_____

_____

_____

_____

_____

2. Our lives have been so filled with events and situations. However, there are a lot of times when we later discover that our perception of those situations was so different from the situation itself. Can you remember one? If so, describe it here, and then describe how you saw it differently from what it actually was.

_____

_____

_____

_____

_____

_____

3. Can I think of a situation where another person's comments affected how I saw myself?

CHAPTER SEVEN:
Why Our Mind Must Fool Us

● ●

"I used to think my brain was the most wonderful organ in my body. But then I thought: Wait a minute, who's telling me that?"
– Comedian Emo Phillips [46]

What We Have Learned So Far

In the last chapter we learned where our self-images come from, and discovered how they are made! Let's briefly summarize enough of the highlights so we can then discover how our self-images can actually *fool* us.

1. What is the self-image? A self-image is simply how you see yourself, especially when you are by yourself with your own thoughts and feelings.

2. We have thousands of self-images. If you are a natural athlete, you probably have a high self-image of yourself as an athlete—higher than in other areas of your life. You may, however, feel weak in the area of finances, so your self-image in the area of financial matters may not be as strong as those who are very comfortable with numbers and calculations.

3. Our self-image is learned. We are born with a "clean slate" in terms of our self-image. In other words, we were not born with a preconceived self-image. Everything that contributes to our self-image has been *learned*, mostly through what we tell ourselves about ourselves (i.e., our self-talk). We have already learned that the comments of others do not affect our self-images unless we agree with them.

4. Although our self-images cannot be replaced, they can be overridden with new ones. Although we can't really *change* our self-images, we will be learning how to override them with new ones. Much of the latter quarter of this book is dedicated to doing just that. In most cases, this overriding can be done rather painlessly, too, without months or years of psychotherapy and drugs.

Why Our Mind Must Fool Us

To truly understand this next section, we must recall the first function of the Creative Subconscious that we discussed in Chapter Five as shown in Figure 1. The function of the creative subconscious is to "make sure that what you do, and how you think, *lines up with your self-image.*" We learned this is also called "Maintaining Sanity."

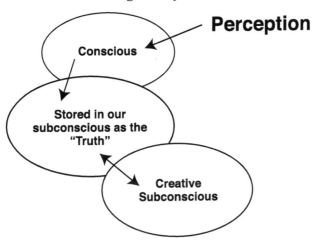

The No. 1 job of the creative subconscious: Maintain sanity

Figure 1

We discovered in the last chapter that your self-image is learned; you were not born with it. And as we saw in my self-image as a child (which said that I could not understood math), a lot of what our self-images learn *is incorrect* (as I am sure you already know!). My self-image about math was based on my self-talk, and that in turn was based on erroneous messages I was accepting from people, and more importantly, *myself*. (*A lot* more on this later.)

As a jumping off point for this chapter, let's look back at what I did as described in the last chapter when I actually got an A on a math test.

> *I remember the only time that I ever got an A on a math test in elementary school. Do you know what I said? "Wow! It must be a mistake!" I did not congratulate myself, nor did I study for the next test. After all, if you are an F student in math, you get F's. You guessed it! I flunked the next math test. Why? Because the "truth" in my self-image was that I could not do math.*

In other words, my creative subconscious was purposely fooling me into believing that I could never do math. The reason is the subject of this chapter.

We'll introduce this subject by adding a new brain principle to our list. (This is the only one we will be considering in this chapter.) This new principle will also show us the reason why Brain Principle One must be true. As you recall, Brain Principle One is: **We behave and act not according to the truth, but the truth as we *believe* or *perceive* it to be!**

Remember, you were not *born* knowing what a car looked like, you learned it through past conditioning. This now leads us to the next brain principle:

Brain Principle Eight

If your past conditioning does not match what you see, your creative subconscious builds a blind spot to it.

Here's an example of this: As a child, my "truth" said that I could not understand math. Receiving an A on a math test did not line up with my past conditioning that I could not understand math. My creative subconscious therefore "fooled" me by telling me that it was a mistake. That is its job—to make sure that how I do in math *lines up with my self-image* of how I should do in math. My self-image was that I was "stupid in math," so the creative subconscious convinced me that my A didn't really count. In other words, my mind **blinded me** to the real truth, for, as I discovered 35 years later, I am brilliant in math.

The Blind Spots We Have In Our Lives

In his seminars, Lou Tice demonstrates the blind spots our brains create with the following card. Read the sentence JUST ONCE, then count the number of F's in the sentence. Then write the number you counted in the square next to the sentence.

FINISHED FILES ARE THE RESULT OF YEARS OF SCIENTIFIC STUDY COMBINED WITH THE EXPERIENCE OF MANY YEARS OF EXPERTS.

When I do this exercise in a workshop, I then ask various students how many F's they counted. Some say two or three or four. Others say as many as seven. When some of the students hear these different numbers, they often hold the cards closer and stare at them with squinted eyes, straining to see all the F's that they somehow are not seeing. While all this is happening, their self-talk is saying things like "I'm so slow!" or "What's wrong with me!" Some students invariably tell me after the workshop how stupid they felt.

Do YOU see all the F's? Actually there are seven of them.

See them? Great! Don't see them? Look for the F's in the word "of." Ahah! There they all are. All seven of them!

Now what just happened here?

Most of us have been taught to read phonetically, based on the sounds a letter makes. The F sound is used in the word "fun." It does not normally sound like the letter "V" like the f sounds in the word "of." So what does the creative subconscious do? *It blocks the "of's" out.* Many of you simply DID NOT SEE those f's in the "of's." The brain actually blinds you from seeing them because they do not line up with the "truth" of how the letter F should sound. This has *nothing* to do with intelligence, or quickness, or how well you read.

Here's the sad part: Say we have a student named Andy who is desperately looking for all of the F's. Especially if there are other students sitting around him who say they see all seven, his self-talk is probably saying things like, "You are SOOOO slow!" or "You're just not as smart!" or "What's wrong with you!" or "You're simply too old for this!" or "You have been out of school too long!" (Believe me, I have heard them all!)

And it doesn't stop there. Andy not only accepts that self-talk, his brain then records these statements as true, contributing (significantly, I might add) to his self-image regarding his intelligence. Even though these statements are *simply not true*, as we have learned, the brain is a literal mechanism; it accepts whatever you tell it as absolutely valid.

How Blind Can We Be?

When we had our first child, a beautiful baby girl named Abigail, we were certain that she was the "perfect" baby. In fact, we made certain the EVERYONE knew that. We had pictures of Abbey in every room in our house, and showed them to all of our unsuspecting friends.

A week later, Mary's mother came to visit. She took one look at Abbey, and said in a very gentle manner, "Dear, Abbey is crossed eyed." We were shocked that she would say such a thing! "She is NOT cross eyed!" we protested. After a few days of disagreeing, we all agreed to take Abbey to a physician to prove grandma wrong.

You already know what the doctor said. Not only were Abbey's eyes crossed, they were both severely crossed. She later had to endure eye patches on both eyes for years, and had several operations. Why didn't we see the crossed eyes? Because we held an image of Abbey being a "perfect" child, and perfect children do not have crossed eyes. Our minds were literally blinded to those crossed eyes.

Try this exercise to demonstrate your own blind spots:

- Hold your hand 12 inches in front of your face.
- Move it 6 inches to the side of your gaze.
- Try counting your fingers while still looking ahead.

Difficult, huh? We do not see the world around us as clearly as we suppose.

Some Problems with Blind Spots

The blind spots which our mind creates bring up some issues.

Issue #1: You don't know where they are.

Lou Tice sums this up very well: "The problem with blind spots is that you don't know where they are. You always think you are seeing the truth. You always think you are hearing the truth. Some of you struggle with college courses and you wonder, 'Am I not smart? Do I not have the aptitude? Is there something wrong with me?' No, chances are pretty good you're very smart, you're very capable, and you just have a blind spot."[47]

I had a blind spot when it came to math. Can you think of places in your life where you have a blind spot?

Issue #2: Everyone has blind spots.

As I reiterated in the last chapter, my oldest sister always seemed to know the answer first in math. I, however, seldom did. For years I thought that, because of this, I must not be very smart. As we discovered, however, it was not that at all. I just had a blind spot for math.

Can We Learn to See Blind Spots?

Absolutely! Although you will always have blind spots, you can learn not only to recognize them, but to watch for them as well. This alone will give you a tremendous advantage over those who have no idea they have blind spots.

Let's do another exercise that demonstrates how quickly you can learn to see a blind spot.

I give my students a card face down and tell them not to look at it until everyone has one. After everyone has the card, I tell them that on the other side of the card is a picture. With that brief comment, I have them turn the card over together. Figure 2 shows you what they see.

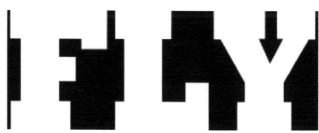

Figure 2

Most people say Figure 2 looks like a bunch of black figures: A top hat on its side on the left, a skinny cigar-store Indian on the right, an arrow pointing down, and so on. Most of the students stare at the card trying hard to see the "picture." I then give them a hint by telling them it is actually a word. After a while, an "Ahah!" emanates from the corner of the room, then another, than another. After enough have seen the word, I tell them that the word is FLY in reversed print. With some of the students, it takes a bit longer to see the word.

While they are struggling though, their self-talk is giving them the same message when they were attempting to see the F's on the "F card" that we looked at earlier in this chapter.

An Encouraging Lesson

After everyone has seen the word FLY, I hand out another card, and again tell them to not turn it over until I give the signal. When they do, they see the following:

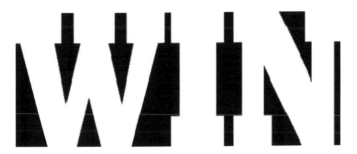

Figure 3

This time they instantly see the word "WIN." I then ask them, "How long did it take you to see the word "WIN?" they all agree it was almost instantaneous. I then point out that this new recognition did not take years of therapy, or reading six self-help books. It simply took a change in their perception—a change in their way of thinking. The smiles that emanate from my students who complete this exercise makes teaching extremely satisfying. Why? Because hundreds of research studies show that when people change their beliefs about something, their emotions and their behaviors can also be significantly overridden.[48] The hope that it brings to my students, and to you as a reader, is so exciting to me.

Next Chapter Preview

In the next chapter we learn about the tremendous impact our attitude has on us and five ways we speak to ourselves.

Remnants to Remember

1. If your past conditioning does not match what you are looking at, your creative subconscious builds a blind spot to it.

2. The challenge with these blind spots is that we often don't know we have them, and we don't know where they are.

 # Points to Ponder

1. What are the benefits of knowing that I have blind spots?

_____

_____

_____

_____

_____

_____

_____

_____

_____

2. Where am I stuck in my life and why? (The way I was raised, where I was raised, my schooling, etc.)

3. What is a blind spot I have had in my life that I am very aware of?

4. What is a blind spot in my life that I have become only recently aware of?

_____

_____

_____

_____

_____

_____

_____

_____

CHAPTER EIGHT:

Learning to Control Your Self-Talk

What We Have Learned So Far

We discovered in the last chapter that although your mind is indeed magnificent, it cannot be completely trusted. This is especially true with your self-images. Why? Because your self-images *have all been learned* in a world that is chaotic at best, and at its worst full of distortions. As a result, we hold distorted self-images ("I cannot understand math!"). This is exacerbated by the fact that your creative subconscious makes sure your behavior lines up with those distorted self-images. As we learned in the last chapter, the brain adds insult to injury by creating blind spots to hide those distortions.

The good news, however, as demonstrated with the FLY and WIN cards at the end of the last chapter, is that we can learn how to change our perceptions, how we think, our self-talk, and as a result our self-images. That is one of the reasons you are reading this book.

Before we move forward, let's examine our self-talk a bit deeper by concentrating on our attitudes, since they come directly from our self-talk. Our attitudes, incidentally, also play a key role in our lives. Ask any employer which is more important, a person's ability or his *attitude*, and they will invariably answer attitude. Why: **Because a person's ability determines if they can do a task; while their attitude determines how well they will do it.**

Where Do Our Attitudes Come From?

We answered part of that question in Chapter Six when we looked at my self-talk and my ability to understand math. I believed that I couldn't understand math. We learned, though, that a belief does not need to be true to be a belief.[49]

The source of our attitudes goes clear back to our self-talk. The progression is as follows:

1. Our self-talk builds beliefs about ourselves. ("I cannot understand math.")
2. Those beliefs control our attitude. ("I *hate* doing math!)
3. Our attitudes control our feelings ("I feel so scared when I have to sit down and do math problems.")
4. The feelings control the actions we'll take. ("I barely study math since I know I am going to flunk it anyway.")

This leads us to **Brain Principle Nine: Our self-talk builds beliefs, our beliefs control our attitude, and our attitude controls our feelings**.

Five Levels of Self-Talk

Since our attitudes go back to our self-talk, it is helpful at this juncture to point out that there are five levels of self-talk. We'll list all five here, talk about the first four briefly, and discuss the last one in detail in Chapter Twelve.

Self-Talk Level 1: Negative Resignation

"I can't do this job!" "This job won't work!" "No way!" When we use negative resignations, the creative subconscious reacts in three ways:

1. It agrees ("OK, if you say so.")
2. It minimizes any energy you might have had to do the job.
3. It actually blocks out options you might have developed to do the job.

SO, BE CAREFUL WHAT YOU SAY, BECAUSE IT WILL MOST LIKELY COME TRUE.

Self-Talk Level #2: But, I'm trying...

A close cousin to "negative resignation" is "But I'm trying..." When a student sits in my office and protests that he is "really trying," I put a stapler (or some other object close at hand) in front of him. I then instruct him to "*try*" to pick up the stapler. His face assumes a very quizzical look. He hesitates for a few seconds, and invariably reaches out to pick up the stapler. "No!" I protest. Don't pick up the stapler. *Try* to pick up the stapler." He sits in front of me for a few more seconds, completely baffled. I then gently tell him that "trying" to do something is completely meaningless. You are either going to do it...or you're not. But saying that you are "trying" to do something is simply a cop-out.

Self-Talk Level 3: The "Shoulds"

I hear this frequently from students trying to break a habit. They say, "I should weigh less!" or "I should be a non-smoker!" or "I *should* be wealthy!"

What they don't understand is that when they make these resolutions, their brain says, "Yeah! You're right! You should! YOU'RE JUST NOT!" The "shoulds" only recognize the problem and have no intention of changing it.

It is interesting to note that our brain *loves* the phrases, "I'm trying..." or "I should..." While they *sound* truly inspirational, these phrases usually bring about *very* little change in your life. And as we will learn, the brain does not *like* to change. It therefore responds to the "shoulds" and the "I'm tryings" with "Good for you! I'm so glad you *are* trying or that you know what you *should* do. Of course, I don't really have any intention of doing any changing at all, but if it makes you feel better when you say these things to yourself, say them for as long as you want. I then don't have to change!"

Self-Talk Level 4: I Quit

This usually takes place after a cataclysmic event has occurred in someone's life, like a death due to cancer. "From now on, I quit smoking!" Of these four, this one usually works best, but it is not by any means the way to truly change on the inside.

Self-Talk Level 5: The Next Time...I Intend To...

We will focus on this level in Chapter Twelve. For now, let me say that this is the way great leaders think, and it is a way you will learn to talk to yourself, especially when you make your next mistake or need to take a step backward before taking a step forward. With this self-talk, you will take what you want in the future and put it into the present NOW! I call this "Creating the Strongest Picture," which we'll look at next, and then learn how to apply it later.

Creating the Strongest Picture

Do you remember when you first learned to ride a bicycle without the training wheels? Your father, mother, brother or sister ran alongside while your hands desperately clung to the steering handles, the bike wobbling every which way. When they finally felt you were ready to ride without their help, they pointed out a rock in the middle of the dirt road 50 feet ahead, and warned you, "Now don't you run into that rock!" Then they gave you a little shove and off you went. To keep yourself from running into that rock, you kept your eyes fastened to it. You know what happened! BAM! Right into the rock!

This illustrates Brain Principle Ten: **Our brains seek the strongest picture**.

We are like a guided missile. Just as a missile seeks objects, we seek pictures or ideas. Unlike a bullet which never veers from its path, however, we are continually correcting ourselves to find whatever target we are searching for. What is that target? Simply the 'strongest picture.' And those strongest pictures are found in your self-images.

For example, when I weighed 230 pounds (back in Chapter Five), my strongest picture (i.e., my self-image) was that of a 230-pound man, because that was who I was. My brain then followed it and never veered away. However, as I began to learn the principles we are learning here, I gradually overwrote that picture to one of being a 200-pound man. (We will learn how to do this in Chapter 13.) As this new picture became the stronger one, I found myself eating and exercising like a 200-pound man. During the next two years, my extra 30 pounds gradually came off.

Your self-talk accomplishes all of this. You must give yourself an idea of what you want to be or become. If you don't, your creative subconscious simply keeps you the way you are, with no change.

Sarah's Story

The best example for understanding how our brains follow the strongest picture is a story about the birth of Sarah, our youngest daughter. When she was being delivered, some severe complications arose, and she was barely breathing. I followed the ambulance as they rushed her to Children's Hospital in San Diego. After Sarah was admitted, the pediatrician examined her—then told me she had about a 50-50 chance of living.

It felt like an arrow had pierced my heart.

Now my sister, Sallee, a perinatal Registered Nurse (RN) who had cared for newborn babies for many years, met me at the hospital. She listened to Sarah's prognosis, then sat me down in the waiting room, looked directly into my eyes (I will never forget this) and declared, "You cannot give up on this child!" I didn't know what she meant. "Sallee," I protested, "She's only three hours old. What do you mean?"

"I mean that it is up to YOU to give Sarah the *desire* to get well," Sallee said. "YOU must paint an amazingly vivid picture of the wonderful place she is going home to, rather than the picture she now has of lying in a perinatal intensive care ward so heavily medicated she cannot move."

"Sallee, she can't even see me or hear me. Sarah probably can't sense my touch! What good can I do?"

"I'll repeat it again, Steve," she said calmly. "It is up to YOU to give her a stronger picture; a picture of your wire-haired fox terrier licking her face when she comes home, of her older sister holding her in that big brown chair, of you and Mary taking her for walks in the park."

So I did what I was told. For the next five days, I stood by Sarah's crib in the hospital talking to her for about 12 hours a day, stroking her back, laughing and such. Yes, I felt kind of foolish because I didn't see how my standing and talking to her could be doing any good.

On about the fourth day, the pediatrician pulled me aside from Sarah's isolette and told me they were at a critical stage in her care. You and I normally breathe about 30 percent oxygen, while Sarah was receiving 100 percent. He told me that over time, this is very destructive, especially to the brain. He said that Sarah must somehow lower her oxygen requirements over the next twelve hours or else they would have to lower the oxygen intake themselves, and then just wait and see. At my wits ends, I went home and brought back my guitar. For the entire night I stood by the isolette singing gentle children's' songs to her, touching her back, talking to her, telling her about her sister Abbey, sharing stories about our dog, Tobe, and telling her about all the wonderful things she could look forward to when she came home.

When they took her blood gas levels the next morning, her oxygen requirements had decreased from 100 percent to 40 percent in 12 hours, and she was home with us three days after that. Wow! Somehow, after her magnificent mind saw a stronger picture at home, it simply said, "Enough of this! I want to go home now and meet my sister!"

This leads us to Brain Principle Eleven. **We move toward and become like that which we think about, and our present thoughts determine our future.** In other words, we move physically and emotionally toward that which we think about.

This is why worrying can be so destructive. I call worrying negative goal setting. When we worry about something (and the events about which we worry seldom happen the way we think they will), we make the worries the strongest picture. Lou Tice points out that Formula One race drivers, the ones in the big speedways, are taught that when their car spins out of control and is heading to the wall, to not look at the wall but instead to look to the "recovery point," the place where they can right the spin. Ordinarily you look where you are going. However, if you keep your eyes fixed on where you are going (in this case, heading toward the wall of the speedway), you will steer your car right into the wall. The discipline becomes this: Even when hurtling toward the wall, keep your focus on where you want to end up.[50]

Worrying also orientates us to the future rather than the present. Besides, almost everything we worry about is uncontrollable or, at least, improbable. We even lead ourselves to believe that somehow through our worrying, we prevent those events from happening. And that only feeds our fears about what "might" happen, especially if we were to stop worrying. We really do worry about not having something to worry about.[51]

I am accident prone. (In fact, I have been called "environmentally challenged.") Although my daughters have been encouraging me for years to buy a cell phone, I *finally* acquired one only a few weeks ago. Why? Because I see myself as having trouble walking without running into walls, much less walking *and* talking on a cell phone. What if every morning before I left the house for work, Mary, my wife, and I would have this conversation:

"Be careful, Steve. Don't walk into any walls. You know how you are!"

"Thanks honey. I had almost forgotten."

"Well, I'm only reminding you because I love you!"

I would then walk into another wall. You see why, right? Because our self-talk truly controls us. This leads to **Brain Principle Twelve: Control your self-talk, or your self-talk will control you**.

This is especially evident when you consider the fact that we think in three dimensions: Past, present, and future. There are those who always think of the "Good Ole Days" (which apparently were really not as good as they say they were), never grow out of them, and resultedly never grow into the future. There are also those "practical" people who only think of the present. They do so because (as they say), "I am just being 'realistic' and 'practical!'" They will always be stuck in the present, and never grow into the future.

It's the "future" dimension that has the most power to change our lives. Studies have shown that significantly successful people always think about the future *as if it has already happened*. Stephen Covey, in his book *7 Habits of Highly Effective People*, calls this "Begin with the End in Mind."[52] We lose weight because we *already* see ourselves as weighing 120, or 140, or 200 pounds, a year before we have actually lost it. *If you are to change, learn, and grow, you will learn to think this way.* You will learn how to make what you want for your future the strongest picture, and the brain will follow it like a guided missile follows a target.

Next Chapter Preview

We will be taking a closer look at some of the crafty ways our mind attempts to hold us back from changing.
By doing so, we can begin to create a foundation for learning how to take back more control of where we want our lives to go.

Remnants to Remember

1. **Brain Principle Nine: Our self-talk builds beliefs, our beliefs affect our attitude, and our attitude affects our feelings.**

2. **Brain Principle Ten: Our brains seek the strongest picture.**

3. **Brain Principle Eleven: We move toward and become like that which we think about, and our present thoughts determine our future.**

4. **Brain Principle Twelve: Control your self-talk, or your self-talk will control you.**

5. There are five levels of self-talk:
   - Negative resignation
   - But I'm trying...
   - I should...
   - I quit, and
   - The Next Time...I Intend to...
     a. We'll concentrate on "The Next Time...I Intend to..." in Chapter Twelve

Points to Ponder

1. What are three attitudes you have about your life that *positively* affect it? Where did they come from?

_____

_____

_____

_____

_____

_____

_____

_____

2. What are three attitudes you have about your life that *negatively* affect it? Where did they come from?

_____

_____

_____

_____

_____

_____

_____

_____

3. Of the five ways we talk to each other, (negative resignation, I am trying…, the Shoulds, I Quit, and The Next Time, I intend to…), which two do you use the most?

_____

_____

_____

_____

_____

_____

_____

_____

4. What are three habits (or attitudes) I want to change in my life?

_____

_____

_____

_____

_____

_____

_____

_____

CHAPTER NINE:
The Reason Change Is So Hard

• •

Let's review the Brain Principles we have learned so far:
1. **We behave and act not according to the truth, but the truth as we *believe* it to be!**
2. **A literal mechanism, the brain accepts what you tell it without argument.**
3. **Our self-talk helps create our self-image.**
4. **Your brain does not record what is happening, but your *version* of what is happening.**
5. **You must agree with the opinion of another about you before it becomes a part of your self-image.**
6. **If your past conditioning does not match what you see, your creative subconscious builds a blind spot to it.**
7. **You are not doomed to the same self-images for your entire life. They can be overwritten!**
8. **Your *own* self-talk has *as much of an affect* on your self-image as what others say to you.**
9. **Our self-talk builds beliefs, our beliefs control our attitude, and our attitude controls our feelings.**
10. **Our brains seek the strongest picture.**
11. **We move toward and become like that which we think about; our present thoughts determine our future.**
12. **Control your self-talk, or your self-talk will control you.**

We have learned a LOT. As this list looks a bit overwhelming, let's reduce them down to two primary principles for this chapter.

Brain Principles 1 through 7 reveal *How Our Mind Works For Us...and Against Us.*

We have learned that as magnificent as your mind is, it is not consistently truthful about what it tells you. Sandra Aamodt, Ph.D., expresses this so well in her book, *Welcome to Your Brain*:[53]

> "*Your brain doesn't intend to lie to you, of course. For the most part, it's doing a great job, working hard to help you survive and accomplish your goals in a complicated world. Because you often have to react quickly to emergencies and opportunities alike, your brain usually aims to get a half-assed answer in a hurry rather than a perfect answer that takes a while to figure out. Combined with the world's complexity, this means that your brain has to take shortcuts and make a lot of assumptions. Your brain's lies are in your best interests—most of the time—but they also lead to predictable mistakes.*"

This is especially true in terms of what your brain tells you about you (i.e., your self-images). Some of your self-images actually have distortions. These distortions come from two sources: Incorrect messages from other people that we accept as fact, and incorrect messages we tell ourselves about ourselves. Remember, the brain accepts all of these messages as completely true, no questions asked. The creative subconscious then makes sure that what you do and how you think lines up with these distorted self-images. Finally, as we learned in Chapter Seven, the brain adds insult to injury by creating blind spots to hide those distortions.

Brain Principles 8 through 12 reveal *How We Can Learn, Grow and Change.*

Your self-images are continually changing, based on whether or not you agree with what other people are telling you about you, or what *you* are telling you about you. Thus, by controlling your self-talk, your self-talk cannot control you. This is tremendously encouraging because it shows us that we CAN change no matter how young or old we are, and can always learn and grow. For this to take place, however, we must learn how to create a stronger picture in our minds of where we want these changes to happen.

So, WHY IS IT SO HARD TO CHANGE?

Of all the questions I receive in my seminars and classes, this question comes up the most, especially by people with longer life experiences. Why is it so hard to change? As we will discover, there are many reasons. I am going to focus on only one here: The creative subconscious.

Remember, research has determined that our ability to learn *depends heavily on our experience, and what we bring to the act of pattern recognition and detection.*[54] *This leads us to our next Brain Principle.*

Brain Principle Thirteen

We base many of our life decisions NOT on what we can do, but on what has happened to us in the past.

All of us can list everything we will never try doing again because of some very unpleasant past memories.

"Wow, I made a fool of myself there."
"I really blew that one!"
"I'll never do THAT again!"

This goes right along with the Garbage-in, Garbage-out principle. Our past can truly limit our future. That is another element we are going to learn to change.

The Wiles of the Creative Subconscious

At this juncture, however, we need to look more closely at the creative subconscious. Why? Because it is the main culprit that keeps us from changing and growing. We are going to expose just one of its crafty ways in this chapter, and later we'll see others. By doing so, we can begin to build a foundation for learning how to take back more control of where we want our lives to go.

Its Job is to Maintain Sanity

As you recall, the primary job of the creative subconscious (it has three jobs; we'll look at the rest later) is *to maintain sanity* by "correcting any mistakes" in our thinking. Remember how I held an image of myself as a 230-pound man, so my creative subconscious regarded losing any weight as a "mistake." It therefore made sure that an entire pecan pie looked absolutely wonderful to eat on a Saturday. "After all," I would say to myself, "I had nothing but carrot juice for lunch all week. I owe it to myself as a reward for being so disciplined!" And back came the pounds.

We can acquire a distinctive picture of what the creative subconscious does by looking at its actions while a person is under hypnosis. A trained hypnotist bypasses a person's conscious and embeds a temporary suggestion in his subconscious. Imagine that after putting you under hypnosis, I tell you that the stapler on the table in front of you weighs 1,000 pounds, and that I will give you $5,000 if you lift it off the table. Now, your self-image for lifting has always known that you cannot lift anything that weighs 1,000 pounds. However, as a college student, you could *really* use the money. You therefore try with all your might to lift the stapler. However, it does not move, try as you might.

Now, just to make sure that you really *are* trying, I attach electrodes to your biceps, the muscles in your arms used for lifting. I then connect the electrodes to an electronic measuring device. The device shows that you really are lifting with about 75 pounds of upward thrust. Still, the stapler does not budge. The stapler *should* be moving—it only weighs a few ounces, and with your 75 pounds of upward force, it should be flying off the table. And yet it doesn't move, no matter how strenuously you try to pick it up.

What is happening? According to the measuring device attached to your biceps, you really are lifting with enough force... and yet the stapler stays still. (I love this exercise, because most of my students cannot determine why the stapler doesn't move.) Then I tell them the secret: I tell them that I will now attach electrodes to your *triceps*—the muscles which act in opposition to your biceps, the muscles in your arms which *push* down. Now, can you now guess why the stapler isn't moving? If not, remember the next sentence, for it will have a *tremendous* affect on your life. For even though you are lifting up with 75 pounds of force to earn $5,000, you are *pushing down* with 75 pounds of force to make sure you can't. Why? Because your self-image "knows" that you cannot lift 1,000 pounds, so your creative subconscious makes you unconsciously push down on a stapler weighing only a few ounces to make sure you don't.

In other words, your creative subconscious counts it as a "mistake" to allow you to lift something as light as a small stapler if your self-image says you cannot, even though you have the physical ability to pick up the stapler with one hand and throw it across the room.

Can you now imagine how much power the creative subconscious has to provide—or limit—what we want to do in life?

Shooting Ourselves in the Foot

The creative subconscious limits us in many ways. In fact, all of us seem to periodically "shoot ourselves in the foot" consciously, or not. A student shared a story with me about a friend of hers who had been an alcoholic for many years. After remaining sober for seven months, her friend began to drink again because, "My life was too good and I could not handle it."

Think of politicians riding at the top of the world, only to be toppled by a sexual indiscretion. When former U.S. Senator, John Edwards was forced to confess his infidelity in 2008, he said, "I started to believe that I was special and became increasingly ego-centric."

I remember the "Smith sisters" at the college where I served as the Evening Dean at the time. These two girls enrolled in our Medical Assistants program. They had come out of a very abusive home, and had lived for a while on the street with all that entails. I interviewed them for quite a while. Their vision was to have careers in drug rehabilitation, since they had been in and out of various drug rehabilitation facilities themselves. Their admissions tests indicated they were extremely intelligent, and the college jumped through hoops to get them admitted. During their first two weeks of class, we met and spoke of their progress each night. On the third week, they burst into my office exclaiming they had both earned A's on their first Medical Terminology exams. This was the first A either of them had ever received at any school. How proud they were of themselves! The next week they earned another A, and another a week after that.

But then their attendance became spotty. I called them every night. At first they provided various excuses. Eventually they stopped the excuses altogether. Soon their phone had been disconnected. Within seven weeks, they had both dropped out of school. I have not seen them since.[a] Why? Because as intelligent as they were, they could not see themselves as successful.

This leads to our final Brain Principle for this chapter.

Brain Principle Fourteen:
We will not allow ourselves to be unlike ourselves.

All of us have the potential to be better. However, when you see yourself as only so good, even though you have the potential to be much better, your creative subconscious always brings you back to the level of where you believe yourself to be (remember, that's its job). If you are absolutely certain that something is going to be really difficult, you will make it hard. When you say, "NO WAY!" the brain simply agrees: "OK, if you say so. You're right; there is no way." However, when you exclaim, "ABSOLUTELY. OF *COURSE* I CAN DO THAT," the brain not only agrees with you, but ACTUALLY ENDEAVORS TO FIND A WAY for you to accomplish what you want to accomplish.

---

[a]Just before this second edition was printed, and three years after the "Smith sisters" had disappeared, I was depositing a check at the bank close to the college where all this had happened. As I handed the check to the teller, she looked at me and exclaimed, "My Campbell! Don't you recognize me! It's Melinda!" It *was* Melinda. She had returned to college long after I had left, gotten her degree, and was getting married that weekend! When I asked about her sister, the look in her face said it all. But there was Melinda, looking so good I hardly recognize her!

Even when we shoot ourselves in the foot, there is ALWAYS a Next Time!.

Making Your Mind Your Mentor

When I began teaching this material to non-college audiences, I used this slogan: Renewing Your Mind by Making It Your Mentor. The dictionary defines a mentor as a "wise and trusted counselor or teacher." One of the objectives of this book then, is to help you do just that.

A mentor is an encourager, one who always sees more in you than you see in yourself.[55] Your mind can be taught how to see what you can become...far before you become it. This involves bringing what you want to be in the future into the present—now—without waiting around for it to somehow happen.

We are getting closer and closer to learning how to do just that.

Next Chapter Preview

We have just learned that your brain will not allow you to be unlike yourself. In the next chapter, we will learn ways to remedy this. So, hold onto your hats, we still have much to learn!

Remnants to Remember

- **Brain Principle Thirteen: We base many of our life decisions NOT on what we can do, but on what has happened to us in the past.**
- **Brain Principle Fourteen: We will not allow ourselves to be unlike ourselves.**

Points to Ponder

1. Briefly describe three ways you have limited yourself because of something that happened in your past.

_____

_____

_____

_____

_____

_____

_____

CHAPTER TEN:

What We Lock Out of Our Lives

• •

What We Have Learned So Far

We are discovering (somewhat to our dismay!) that our wonderful brain is, in one sense, not so wonderful. In fact, it cannot always be trusted. By the time you finish this book, you will have become (I hope!) a healthy skeptic about which messages you agree with when your mind talks to you.

When we learned in the last chapter that **the brain will not allow you to be unlike yourself,** we also discovered just how far it will go to prevent that from happening. Under hypnosis, your brain purposely holds you back from picking up a 10-ounce stapler because your self-image has been hypnotized into thinking you cannot.

But it doesn't stop there! Your mind also holds you back from learning, growing and changing when these changes make you unlike yourself. This is the reason that *all* of us periodically shoot ourselves in the foot. The creative subconscious will do almost anything in its power to prevent us from becoming unlike ourselves. Don't worry, though—there are many ways to remedy this, and we will be learning the most effective ones.

Let's begin with the next Brain Principle:

Brain Principle Fifteen:
The Brain Would Rather Flee Than Change.

In this chapter we are going to look at *another* method the brain uses to prevent change in your life. When your dreams are coming true, or you are growing too much, or too fast, your brain usually wants to retreat, or lower your expectations, or convince you to accept less of yourself. It does this very craftily, however, by masquerading its fear by emphasizing the need for you to be "more realistic." It does this by telling you that lowering your expectations is really a "*good* thing" because after all, you need to be "practical" about these things. Other messages your brain loves are:

- "Maybe I'm taking on too much."
- "I've *never* been able to do that. Why try now?"
- "I'm just not smart enough"
- "I've been out of school too long."
- "I'm just too old!"
- "I have always weighed too much."
- "I have always been too skinny."

I have heard all of these from my students. And here's one of the brain's favorites: "HOW am I going to do that? What in the world was I thinking!?" (Chapter 17 will teach you how to deal with *that* ploy.)

Let's see now how your brain actually locks out change.

The Lock-on/Lock-out Principle

To demonstrate the Lock-on/Lock-out principle to my students, I divide them into pairs. I instruct them to close their eyes, then remember the steps they took to prepare for school that morning. This might have involved exercising, making breakfast, or preparing their children for school. It also might have involved reading the paper, ironing a shirt, or taking a shower. After about a minute, I instruct them to open their eyes and turn their chairs so that each pair directly faces the other.

With each person looking at the other feeling a bit awkward, I tell them that, at the count of three, one partner will describe the steps he or she took to get ready for school. I also tell them that the other partner will do the same AT THE SAME TIME! In other words, *both* partners will be describing how they prepared for the day at the same time. I then tell them that after about 5 minutes, the first partner in a pair will describe to the other what the second partner had said, and then the second partner will repeat what the first partner had said.

When I give these instructions, an audible groan wells up in the room, for they sense what is coming. At the count of three, utter pandemonium fills the classroom as *everyone* attempts to describe their day to their partner and simultaneously listen to their partner. After just a few seconds, I see everyone talking loudly, laughing, smiling, and shaking their heads in frustration. After about 30 seconds (I lie about giving them five minutes to do this) I instruct everyone to stop talking. We then discuss what just happened.

They have discovered that they cannot talk and listen at the same time. Their brain had to make a decision: It had to either concentrate on what they were saying, or concentrate on their partner's comments, *but it could not do both at the same time.* The brain simply had too much to take in. My students discover through this exercise that they had to lock-on to their own talking while locking-out that of their partner's, or vice-versa. This is called the Lock-On/Lock Out principle.

An excellent example of this principle is Cliff Young, the Australian runner we met in Chapter Four. While the other marathoners were locked-on to sleeping, Cliff locked-on to NOT sleeping, and kept running. Recent studies have shown that people who begin to talk about the possibility of divorce (in other words, they "lock-on"), often find themselves proceeding inevitably in the direction of divorce.[56]

The Young Lady/Old Lady card

I also use the Young Lady/Old Lady card to demonstrate this principle. This is found in innumerable psychology books and magazines. Look at Figure 1 below:

Figure 1

I hand out a card to each student and ask them what they see. Many see a picture of a young lady with a feather sticking out of her hair, looking over her right shoulder. Others see a picture of an old lady with a large nose looking down. Others say they cannot see anything at all. After a few moments, however, various "Ahah's!" begin to emanate from different sections of the classroom as a student spots either the young lady or the old lady. I then inform them that the card actually has both, and instruct them to keep looking until they can see both of them.

While the students search for the ladies, I warn them to be very careful about what their brains are saying to them as they search. This is in fact where students (and you) must become the skeptics that I referred to at the beginning of this chapter. If a student can only see the young lady, while others see the old, or if the opposite is true, the student's brain becomes very fearful, and begins whispering little messages to him such as "Boy, look at how fast *she* found it! You are SOOO slow!" Or, "You really can't see her can you?" or "This is so typical of you. You never *could* do these kinds of puzzles. What's wrong with you?!"

We have already learned that those messages do not become a part of our self-image until we agree with them. Hopefully, by this time, you are beginning to learn how NOT to listen to those messages. Rather than saying, "I am *so stupid* because I can't see the young lady, or the old lady, or any lady at all!" you are learning to simply say to yourself, "I have not seen her yet, but I will…just give me some more time!" (We'll learn how to change to this kind of self-talk in Chapter 13.)

One at a Time

There is another interesting psychological phenomenon taking place here: The students who first see the young lady *cannot* see the other lady, for their brains have 'locked' onto the young one, and locked *out* the old one. (If they first see the old lady, the opposite is true.) This illustrates the fact that the brain can initially perceive only one thing at a time, just like a computer. (While a computer seems to be doing many functions at once, actually it performs only one function at a time—but performs each function very, very quickly.)

It goes further, though. When you lock-on to "I'm so dumb at this," you lock out your ability to do it![57] Although this is a sample of Negative Resignation which we discussed in Chapter Eight, the Lock-on/Lock-out principle reveals how tremendously debilitating Negative Resignation can really be. When a person says "No way!" they actually lock-out the way. The first time the Australian marathoners raced with Cliff Young, they locked-on to their "obvious" need for sleep, and lost the race to Cliff by a day and a half! When they raced the second year, though, all of them had learned how to lock-on to needing no sleep, and they beat Cliff's record that year...and the year after that!

Can you see how encouraging this can be? It opens up all sorts of possibilities about locking-on to new changes in our lives, and locking-out those habits that we have been trying to rid ourselves for years. We really *can* change what we lock-on to, and what we lock-out. In other words, if you lock-on to the wrong information, guess what you lock out? The right information.[58]

All of this brings us back to blind spots, and the fact that we are so unaware of them. Younger people in particular have a harder time believing this, for their naiveté makes them so certain that what they are hearing and seeing is the absolute truth. Older people, however, have an easier time accepting blind spots, for with age comes less and less certainty that they are always seeing the truth. Wisdom truly does come with age.

Does this mean that locking-on and locking-out are bad? Absolutely not! When we learn how to set and consistently meet our goals in Chapter 17, we must first learn that in order to truly change, we *must* lock-on to those goals *as if they have already happened*!

Bringing the Future into the Present

At the college where I once taught, the President of the college came into my class of new students the first week. He had each student put on a graduation gown, took a picture of them in the gown, and handed each student that picture. With that picture came an immediate vision of how they will look at their graduation ceremony. These pictures would usually end up on students' refrigerators or mirrors at home, so they could lock-on to their graduation daily by simply looking at them and imagining themselves as *already* graduated.

Do you remember how the brain always follows the 'stronger picture?' Just like those students in their graduation gowns, your mind must be given a stronger picture of what you want the changes in your life to be. The reason change is so difficult is that our 'stronger picture' is almost always the way we are *now*, AND THAT IS WHAT THE BRAIN FOLLOWS! We therefore must learn how to bring the future changes we want in our lives into the present...*now...as if they have already happened*. We will be learning how to do this in Chapters 14 and 15.

Wow, we are getting so close...

Next Chapter Preview

Our brains are actually wired in a way that makes "great" a difficult status to maintain. And although we cannot change that wiring, we can override it by making what we want in our lives such predominant pictures that the brain fastens onto them just like the little boy fastened onto the rock when he was learning how to ride a bike. We will learn about how to create those stronger pictures next.

Remnants to Remember

- **Brain Principle Fifteen: The Brain Would Rather Flee Than Change**
- **The Lock-On/Lock-Out Principle**
  - When confronted with new information that is very different from what it already knows, the brain must sometimes make a decision. It must accept the new information and block out the old, or reject the old information and accept the new. It cannot easily accept both.
- **A Deeper Look at Negative Resignation**
  - The Lock-On/Lock-Out Principle goes a bit further though, Locking onto a statement or a principle such as "I cannot do this," can lock out the possibility of actually doing it.
  - This is a sample of negative resignation that we discussed in Chapter Eight, and the lock-on/lock-out principle reveals how tremendously debilitating negative resignation can really be.
- **Bringing the Future into the Present**
  - Not only is our mind able to project into the future, it can bring the future into the present. This simply means that you can imagine a goal being reached, before you have reached it.
- **Following the Strongest Picture**
  - The brain always follows the 'stronger picture' as illustrated by running into the rock when we keep our eyes fastened on it. We will be using this a great deal as we learn how to make our mind our greatest motivator.

Points to Ponder

1. Briefly describe two times in your life when you locked out opportunities because you did not think you had what you needed to reach them.

2. Based on what you have learned in this chapter, describe how you would react differently to these opportunities?

3. Briefly describe two dreams/visions/goals that you see in the future that you would like to bring into the present. (We will be learning how to do just that.)

CHAPTER ELEVEN:

We Remember What We Value

• •

There will always be a conflict between good, great, and possible.
–Henry Martyn Leland

Staying 'Great' is Difficul

History has repeatedly shown achieving greatness often holds the seeds of its own downfall.[59] In his book *Get Out of Your Own Way*,[60] Robert Cooper tells the story of touring Rome with a guide who pointed out one marvelous achievement after another of the first Roman emperor, Augustus. As they marveled at the remnants of Augustus's grand designs, the guide exclaimed with pride that this era marked the pinnacle of Rome's greatness. Robert asked what happened next. After an awkward pause, the guide said, "Slow ruin."

While this is an extreme example, the same can be said for individuals, groups, and organizations.[61] *Forbes* magazine annually names a Company of the Year based on past performance and projected staying power. However, since 1995 more than half of those honored suffered tremendous declines almost immediately after being named.[62] Large corporations also shoot themselves in the foot. From what we have learned so far, it doesn't require an astrophysicist to guess the reason: Corporations are run by people, and people are run by their brains.

Jim Collins begins chapter one of his book *Good to Great* with the following:

> *"Good is the enemy of great. And that is one of the key reasons why we have so little that becomes great. We don't have great schools, principally because we have good schools. We don't have great government, principally because we have good government. Few people attain great lives, in large part because it is just so easy to settle for a good life."* [63]

The Amygdala and the Reticular Activating System

From what we have learned so far, we can guess that our settling for just being "good" comes from our brain. In this chapter, we will be examining the affects of two specific neurological components within the brain that work in tandem with one another. What they accomplish together is very interesting.

The first is an almond-shaped group of neurons located deep in the brain called the *amygdala* (the dark circles in Figure 1). The other, shown in Figure 2, is a network of cells called the *reticular formation*, also called the *reticular activating system*, which we'll refer to as the RAS. The amygdala has the primary role of processing and memory of emotions,while the RAS allows only information into your brain that you deem valuable.

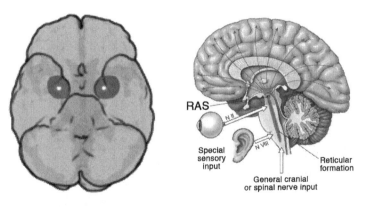

Figure 1   Figure 2

Our brains are actually wired in a way that makes "great" a difficult status to maintain. The amygdala thrives on routine. It is the reason our brains would rather flee than fight, as we learned in Chapter Ten. In fact, the amygdala scans everything that happens to you, or could happen to you, moment to moment, ever alert for even a hint of change in your normal patterns. When it detects such a change, it floods you with warnings about the dangers of what you are doing.[66]

The amygdala works in concert with the reticular activating system. The RAS sits as a gatekeeper at the base of your brain atop the spinal cord.[67] Of its many functions, the one that interests us the most about the RAS is its *filtering* system. The best way to understand how this filtering system works is through a number of illustrations.

Consider the relationship between a mother and her newborn baby. That mother can sleep in a room with trucks roaring by on the street outside, or jets screaming overhead, yet will usually sleep through both. However, if her baby in the crib next to the bed, or even in the next room wakes up with the whisper of a cough, the mother instantly snaps awake!

What is the difference between the jets screaming overhead, and the baby's cough? The answer can be summed up in one word: *Value*. The mother immediately wakes up because she places infinitely more value on her child than on the jet. And because of this, her brain is continually tuned into her baby because of the value she holds for that precious child. It is not the loudness that gets through, it is the value.

Here's another example: Say you are shopping in the busiest section of town during the Christmas shopping season, so you have placed a very high value on finding a parking space. As you drive around the streets chatting with your friend seated next to you, your brain is constantly watching for people with shopping bags walking on the sidewalk, or parking lights going on, or exhaust spewing out of a car, or shoppers loading bags in their trunks. None of these are empty parking spaces, but your brain knows they soon will be, and hones in on them. Again, this happens because you have placed a value on finding a parking space.

A third example: You decide to go shopping for a gift for a friend's, but you start off saying, "I'm going to get him *something* for his birthday." You then spend the *entire* day looking for something and find *nothing*? The reason is because there are so many "somethings" that you find nothing! You do not know what you are looking for, so sure enough, you find nothing! We have all faced that frustration.

If, however, you say, *I am looking for such-and-such a watch, with this type of band, with these specific features, and in this price range*, you will find that watch in all the stores. Why? Because you have placed a *value* on what you are looking for.

A fourth example: You are looking for a new toaster with specific features in a particular price range. You open the paper at breakfast and spot a sale at a particular department store for the very toaster you want! You turn the page—another store has a sale for the same toaster! And look! There's another one in your favorite shopping center! Now, were you just lucky? Did you just happen to turn to the right pages at the right time and find all the sales? No! Your brain honed in on them because you placed a *value* on what you are looking for.

These examples simply show how amazing the RAS acts as a filtering system. It must be, because so much information hits our senses throughout the day—think of all the lights, sounds, smells and so on. We saw that demonstrated when I told you about the exercise in my classroom where pairs of students must talk to each other at the same time about how they prepared for class that morning. Their brains HAD to decide whether to lock-on or lock-out. There was just too much information.

Have you ever begun reading a book, and found yourself having to read the first page three times before it begins to sink in? When this happens, we say one of two things: The material is dull or difficult, or we pass ourselves off as simply being slow to understand. Again, the reason we had to read that first page several times usually does *not* lie in the material or our intelligence! It lies in the material having no importance to us. The

RAS filters out the information that you deem unimportant. The only information it lets through, like the baby's cough, like the parking space, like the toaster, is the information you believe as important.

The WHY and WIIFM Questions

It is for this reason my college students continually ask two questions of every course they take. I call them the **WHY** and **WIIFM** (pronounced "wif-ehm") questions.

WHY am I studying this material?

What's **I**n **I**t **F**or **M**e?

The answer to these questions plays a significant part in how well students understand a course. Why? Because if they do not understand the reason for taking a course, no matter how intensely they study, *very little will get through*. Let me show you this in real life, by telling you Abigail's story.

Abigail's Story

Although Abigail loved the social part of high school, most of her classes bored her, and she barely made it through her senior year. At the beginning of that last year, I took her to a "Daddy-Daughter" luncheon, where we talked about her future. During lunch, she told me that she didn't ever want to go to college, but instead wanted to go to Hollywood to become an actress. So...after a lot of discussion, we rented a truck and helped her move to Hollywood.

After living there for many years, she acquired a job as a writing assistant for a very popular television show; serving the writers coffee and donuts, and making copies of the scripts. She eventually called us and said, "You know...If I don't go to school, I'm going to be serving coffee and donuts the rest of my life." We just listened.

Two years later, she called us again to say how much she loved to write, and would it be alright if she went to a junior college in southern California for a year. (This was the same person who had been completely bored by school.) She finished that first year, called us again, and asked if she could move back up to northern California and live with us while she attended a junior college in northern California.

So, we rented another truck and moved her back up, repainted her old room, and she attended the junior college while living with us. We quickly discovered that when she was studying, you did NOT want to be the person who walked into her room unannounced!

Two years later, we attended her graduation from the University of California at Berkeley, where she graduated with a 4.0 in English.

Now, think about this: Did those nine years in Hollywood suddenly make Abigail smart? Of course not! She had always been smart! Instead, she came to see the *value* of going to college, and once she did that, her brain found ways for her to succeed at one of the top universities in the world!

The Importance of Goals

Chapter 17 will examine in detail how the brain becomes our greatest fan for meeting our life goals. Since the reticular activating system is profoundly involved, this is a good place to begin looking at the importance of goals.

The brain has an interesting response when it comes to meeting goals. We talked about your brain constantly searching for parking spaces in the busiest section of town during the Christmas shopping season. In the same way, the brain constantly looks for ways to help meet the goals you have set for your life. However, when you have no goals, the reticular activating system doesn't know what information *is* important, and therefore filters out what might have helped you meet those goals. Our brains block out information that it believes (often erroneously) is not important.

Let's return to Abigail to see a perfect example of this phenomenon. The student housing in Berkeley, Calif., is inadequate at best; finding a place to live each year can be a student's greatest challenge. However, Abigail's brain found a way. During her last year, a girlfriend told her about a classic Victorian house nestled up in the Berkeley Hills. The owner was never home, so every year she interviewed and selected one college student to live in her house free-of-charge in exchange for taking care of her house and her dog. Abigail was chosen, so her last year of college at U.C. Berkeley was rent-free.

The brain truly does find a way!

Here comes a key, key point: Who decides what is significant? You do! The goals you make for yourself open up your awareness of what *you* deem as important. As a result, your brain looks for information to help meet your goals. Put another way, the *goal* comes first, and then your brain acts as a motivator to help you meet that goal. This is what your brain will do for you!

We will be learning how to very soon.

Next Chapter Preview

Although the importance of our self-talk has run like a thread throughout the book, the next chapter will teach us about the Self-Talk—Self-image Cycle that can easily hang us up. The remaining chapters will then teach us how to get out of this Cycle. We will also examine The Next Time far deeper so it can become a permanent part of our thinking.

Remnants to Remember

- Staying 'Great' is difficult.
  - Our brains are actually wired in a way that makes staying great difficult.
- The Reticular Activating System (The RAS)
  - RAS is a network of cells starting at the base of your brain acting as an amazing filtering system. There is simply so much information hitting our senses throughout the day that your brain must selectively lock some of it out and allow some it in.

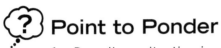 **Point to Ponder**

1. Describe a situation in your life where you felt the same as Einstein described when he said, "How many people are trapped in their everyday habits; part numb, part frightened, and part indifferent? To have a better life, we must keep choosing how we are living."[68]

CHAPTER TWELVE:

What Your Self-Talk Says to Your Self-Image

• •

This chapter could also be called The Ubiquitous Self-Talk—Self-Image Cycle. I use the word "ubiquitous" to impress my colleagues (and it *always* does); it simply means "being everywhere," like electricity, telephones, and now in the 21st Century, computers. However, ubiquitous also can refer to a pattern that all human beings follow. This especially pertains to a mental pattern called the **Self-Talk—Self-Image Cycle**. To understand it, however, we again need a brief review of some of the psychological highlights we have learned.

A Review of the Highlights

In previous chapters we discovered that our brain cannot always be trusted to tell the truth. It will, we learned, do anything to ensure that our self-images match what we are doing. This is the reason that change can be so difficult.

We then learned in the last chapter that a part of the brain called the reticular activating system (RAS) allows only information into your brain that you deem as important or valuable, like the baby's cough, or the parking space in a crowded section of the city. We also learned the reverse is true: The RAS also filters *out* information that you deem *un*important, or insignificant. For example, imagine that after dialing "411" for a specific telephone number, the recording quotes you the number as "560-5466." After hanging up the phone, you silently repeat the number over and over to yourself so you'll remember it enough to dial it. If someone inadvertently enters the room, you yell out, "Don't talk to me! Don't talk to me!" as you frantically dial the number before you forget it. As soon as someone answers on the other end, what happens to 560-5466? It immediately disappears from your mind because it is no longer needed.

We then related this to the importance of goals: Without goals, your brain does not know what you deem as important. It therefore does not know what to keep, and what to filter out. More about that in Chapter 17.

The Self-Talk and the Self-Image Cycle

Although the importance of our self-talk has run like a thread throughout the book, we are now ready to learn about the Self-Talk—Self-Image Cycle.

Let's begin by remembering that your subconscious accepts everything you tell it, without question. We learned in Chapter Five that when you say "I can't do it!" your brain says, "OK You can't." When you have a huge yawn and exclaim how tired you are, the brain says, "OK I didn't know that, but I'll make sure you feel that way." This is a universal principle. Think you're getting a cold? Watch out, you've got it. Think you're getting a headache? It's yours. Think you're going to have a rough day at work? You own it! Think your kids are going to act up at grandma's house? Never fails.[69]

We have also learned that we have thousands of self-images, and each one is simply your opinion of yourself recorded in your subconscious. These self-images aren't necessarily factual; they are simply opinions of how athletic you see yourself, how smart you are, how shy you are, how politically savvy you are, and so on.

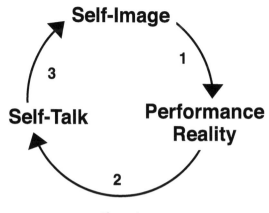

Figure 1

How were these self-images formed? We have already learned that you were not born with them; they have been learned by assimilating your self-talk. Your brain then creates new self-images when you acquire a new habit or skill, or modifies your existing self-images as your brain listens to your self-talk. This alone reveals the encouraging fact that our self-images are continually changing, and can therefore be *overwritten*! This is known as *neuroplasticity*.

Figure 1 shows how we get caught in the Self-Talk—Self-Image cycle. We already have established that your self-image affects how you act. How you act is called your "Performance Reality." The Australian marathon runner Cliff Young had a self-image of a person who did not sleep while running the Sydney to Melbourne Marathon. His Performance Reality was therefore one of not sleeping. We have learned that when I say, "I can't do it!" the brain agrees, and your Performance Reality is usually blocked from your doing it. When you say, "Of course I can do it!" the brain agrees with that, too, and your Performance Reality finds a way of doing it.

Another way of expressing this is that your self-image affects your actions (named your Performance Reality), as indicated by the arrow marked with a (1) in Figure 1.

Your Performance Reality then affects what you say to yourself. One of the reasons I thought I was bad at math was because my Performance Reality was one of continually failing math tests, and getting F's on my homework. Whenever I saw that F, my self-talk said, "I can't do math." In other words, how I do something directly affects my self-talk about my ability to do it. This is illustrated by the arrow marked with a (2).

The cycle is completed by the fact that what really shapes your self-image, and always has, is your self-talk—how you've talked to yourself.[70] This is diagramed by the arrow marked with a (3).

So when my self-image was one who did badly in math, my Performance Reality kept me flunking my math tests (1). Whenever I did, my self-talk said, "And you're surprised? You've never been good at math." (2). My self-image was then lowered even further in the area of math (3). I then kept flunking more math tests, and the cycle simply repeated itself.

This cycle illustrates one reason that change is so difficult. It also illustrates the fact that many of us evaluate ourselves based on what we say about ourselves, or what others say about us. A lot of us are frequently asking ourselves "Did I do well?" or "Did I do poorly?"

When we do poorly, we often say to ourselves, "Well, that's not surprising! I have never been good at that!"

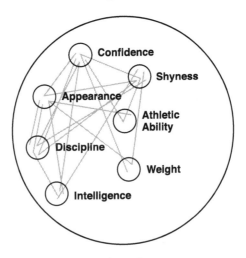

Figure 2

When we say that, another image has been laid down and connected to the patterns of self-images that are stored in our subconscious, as shown in Figure 2. In other words, your self-talk, which is going on continually, either strengthens what you know about yourself, or lowers it. And it is this self-talk that forms your self-image, which in turn affects what you do.

The brain also endeavors to keep us in this cycle. In Chapter Five, I told of my reaction when I got an A on a math test. Starting with my self-image that I am terrible at math, the cycle goes something like this:

>**Self-Image** "I am terrible at math!"
>
>**Performance Reality** I get an A on a math test.
>
>**Self-Talk** "It's gotta be a mistake. I *never* get an A on a math test.
>
>**Self-Image** "Since the A was obviously a mistake, I am still terrible at math!"
>
>**Performance Reality** I *flunk* the next math test.

Many of us habitually reject successes in our lives. In fact, this cycle keeps us "dumb" when we aren't, or poor when we don't need to be. The creative subconscious's job is to make you act like your present self-image—not your potential but like your present self-image.[71]

Can we escape this cycle?

Absolutely. There are two ways. The most effective one, which is long-term, is taught in the next three chapters. The second way happens by simply thinking differently when you make a mistake, undermine yourself, or shoot yourself in the foot. We touched on this in Chapter Eight when we looked at the five levels of self talk. They were **Negative Resignation, But I'm trying..., The "Shoulds," I Quit**, and **The Next Time...I Intend To...**

The Next Time…I Intend To…

I will now concentrate on "**The Next Time…I Intend To…**" This involves *insisting* on seeing yourself and what you do differently. From now on, when you make your next mistake today, or undermine yourself, or shoot yourself in the foot, *think differently than you have before* by following these three steps:

1. If necessary, make a mental note of your mistake and learn from it,

2. Feel *really* bad…*for no more than 15 seconds*, and

3. then say "**That is not like me anymore. The next time, I intend to….**" and create a picture in your mind of how you want to be the next time. (We will learn *how* to do this meticulously in the next two chapters.)

The phrase **The Next Time** has three encouraging inferences.

1. There will *always* be another Next Time.

When I ask my students how many "next times" they have, usually the room becomes quiet, and I see some puzzled looks. After a few moments, however, one or two students exclaim, "There *are* no limits!"

Correct!

As long as we are alive, there is *always* a next time; they *never* run out. Unfortunately, most of us weren't born with this mind-set. Even the great leaders (who live and breathe this mind-set) by their own admission also had to learn this.

2. Always having a "Next Time" can be encouraging.

When I awake in the morning, I always say to myself, "Oh, boy, another chance! I get another Next Time." Having another chance means that room for learning and growing and changing *still* exists.

3. "The Next Time" is a far healthier reaction!

We will learn in Chapter 17 that without goals, people die. "The Next Time" however, opens you up to new goals and reasons to grow and learn and change. Lou Pace has a wonderful observation. He writes:

"This is also theologically sound, not just psychologically sound. It you do something that offends somebody or offends God, you ask forgiveness of God. If you look at the sacrament of penance, it is just, "Go and sin no more. Do it right the next time." You must give yourself a picture in your mind of the way you choose to be, the way you want your life to be, the way you want your behavior to be. See, you need to have something teleologically to see. So you shut off the negative, and you give yourself the positive. This is the way high performance people work and operate in their mind." [72]

You will learn *exactly* how to do this in the next two chapters, because now you are ready.

Tonya's Story

When I taught this principle to a career transitions class a number of years ago, a student named Tonya stopped me one day in the hall with a brightness in her eyes I had never seen before. She told me that for years when she and her husband argued, they would tear each other down emotionally. They had started an argument after she had arrived home after learning this principle. When he began tearing into her (as always), she held her hand up and quietly declared, "Stop! That is not like me anymore!" Her husband stared at her with a *very* puzzled look in his eyes. When he began to tear into her again, she repeated the same statement. (She had to do this three more times!) Finally, the anger between both of them gradually subsided, and they began centering on the *issue*, rather than each other. In time, the husband in turn learned to protect his own self-image by not allowing *her* to tear into *him*.

I saw her about six months after she had graduated, and she told me that their arguing has taken a complete turn around. They still argue at times, but now, as she said, they "fight fair." It has also helped their relationship immensely.

Steven's Story

At one point in my life I taught college during the day and then in the evening served as the school's Evening Dean. Even though I loved my work, the long days sometimes did tire me out. One day I had just purchased a wallet at a large shopping mall and was walking back to my car just as the sun was setting. A few seconds after I stepped off the curb into the parking lot, I heard and felt a huge "WUUMPH!!" in the small of my back, and found myself flying in the air. I then heard a girl scream, "Oh, my God, I've hit someone, I hit someone!" As I lay face down on the parking lot, I said to myself, "I think I've been hit by a car."

The next voice I heard said to me, "Hello. My name is Alma and I'm a paramedic. I've already called for the ambulance and it's on its way. Don't move. You'll be alright!"

As I lay there on my stomach, my first thought was, "Wait a minute. I can't be hurt! I've got my favorite class to teach tomorrow!" (That class is the one you are learning in this book.) I then thought that my wife, Mary, should know that I just got hit by a car, so I lifted my head slightly and asked Alma to call my wife, and gave her Mary's cell phone number. I also asked Alma to call the college and tell them that I wouldn't be at work that night.

When the ambulance arrived, they bundled me up and rushed me to the hospital. As we drove, the paramedics checked my vitals, started an IV, and asked me various questions to determine my lucidity. After determining I was stable, one of the paramedics exclaimed, "Wow! You really did a number on that car!" When I asked what she meant, she said that the entire front of the car was smashed in, including the windshield. "With what?" I asked. She exclaimed, "With the back of your head!"

When Mary and our daughter, Sarah, arrived at the hospital, they were told that they could not see me until I had been examined by the attending physician. They were then led into a waiting room. In the meantime, the physician came in to see me. He poked and prodded, and kept asking me, "Does this hurt?" I said no to all his prods and pokes. He examined my X-rays, then went to see Mary. "Well," the doctor said, "Your husband should be either *really* hurt. Or, he should be..." He didn't finish the sentence. "But he's not!" he said. "In fact, we can't see anything wrong. So you can take him home."

I taught my class the following Monday (heavily medicated, but hey, I made it through!).

What happened?

The driver who did not see me in the setting sun was driving about 20 miles per hour. The doctor said that I would have been seriously hurt if she had been driving a bit faster. I am a jogger (albeit a *very* slow one), so I am moderately in shape. I never saw her coming, so my body was relaxed when the car hit me. But more than any of this, as I lay splayed on the parking lot, my very first thought was, "I don't have time for this! I've gotta teach tomorrow!" My brain's strongest picture wasn't a hospital bed, but rather standing in front of a classroom teaching what I am teaching you now.

There is, indeed, *always* a next time.

 ## Next Chapter Preview

The next chapter is not really a chapter at all. Instead, it's a benchmark we have now reached that will summarize what we have learned so far.

 ## Remnants to Remember

- **The Self-Talk and the Self-Image Cycle**
  - This cycle illustrates why change is so difficult. It also illustrates the fact that many of us are frequently judging ourselves based on or what we say about ourselves, or what others say about us. A lot of us are frequently asking ourselves "Did I do well?" or "Did I do poorly?
- **"From Now On...I Intend To..."** This is a response we can make when we make a mistake. It involves insisting on seeing yourself and what you do...differently.

Points to Ponder

1. Describe a situation in which you found yourself in the Self-Talk—Self-Image Cycle.

   _____
   _____
   _____
   _____
   _____
   _____
   _____
   _____

2. Describe a mistake you made in which "The Next Time, I Intend to…" would have been a better response. Describe what you would have done "the next time."

   _____
   _____
   _____
   _____
   _____
   _____
   _____

YOUR FIRST BENCHMARK

You have reached the first of two benchmarks, so we are now ready to go onto the second phase of your learning how to make your mind magnificent! This first benchmark can be summed up this way:

The brain works magnificently...both for us and against us.

Through the 15 brain principles we have learned (listed at the end of this brief section for your convenience), we have discovered that our brain is indeed magnificent, and its ability to learn and grow and change is virtually limitless. However, we also have learned that it **does not like change**. In fact, its *job* is to make sure that what you do and how you think lines up with your self-images, even if some of those self-images are self-destructive. In other words, **Your brain will not let you be unlike yourself**. Actually, it would be just as content to have you pass the time watching some mindless television show while you munch on a cheeseburger and some fries. The more it can run on preprogrammed routines and habits, without glancing far above your shoe tops as you watch TV, the happier your brain is—and the more it is actually in your way.[73] In fact, most of us have already discovered that we often want "this" while our brain wants "that"—and that our brain almost always wins. We also have learned that in adverse circumstances, your brain inherently wants you to retreat, lower your expectations, and accept less from yourself, and your life.[74]

So although your brain truly is magnificent, it must be taught to play the tune that *YOU* want. In the process of teaching it this, you will be learning that, *and remember this forever*:

Your brain is both reactive and proactive.

Up to this point, we have been examining its **reactive** element. We have been discovering its reaction to change, and the fact that your brain does not like change, and when it can, it holds you back. We are now ready to discover its *proactive* element, and we will be doing so in this next section by exploring "Affirmations."

A Confession

When I first learned about the concept of affirmations many years ago, I was *very* dubious. Having a scientific background, I did not believe (and I still do not believe; more on that later) that if you simply repeat an affirmation over and over, your dreams will come true, or changes will take place in your life, or your self-images will become different. Studies have demonstrated over and over however, that, affirmations do work, **if they are done correctly**. Studies have also demonstrated that your mind can become your greatest support and motivator. We will discover this by first learning in the next chapter just how and why affirmations work from the perspective of your mind, and then how to actually create and imprint them in the following chapters. However, what we learn will *always* be in the context of **how the brain reacts and what it does with affirmations**. In the process, you will also be learning that your mind *can* become your greatest motivator.

The First Fifteen Brain Principles

1. We behave and act not according to the truth, but the truth as we believe it to be!
2. The brain is a literal mechanism that accepts what you tell it without argument.
3. Our self-image is based on our self-talk.
4. Your brain is not recording what is happening, but your version of what is happening.
5. You must agree with the opinion of another about you before it becomes a part of your self-image.
6. If your past conditioning does not match what you see, your creative subconscious builds a blind spot to it.
7. You are not doomed to the same self-images for your entire life. They can be overwritten!
8. Your own self-talk has as much an affect on your self-image as what others say to you.
9. Our self-talk builds beliefs, our beliefs control our attitude, and our attitude controls our feelings.
10. Our brains seek the strongest picture.
11. We move toward and become like that which we think about, and our present thoughts determine our future.
12. Control your self-talk, or your self-talk will control you.
13. We base almost all of our life decisions NOT on what we can do, but on what has happened to us in the past.
14. We will not allow ourselves to be unlike ourselves.
15. The brain would rather flee than change.

CHAPTER THIRTEEN:
Your Subconscious and Your Comfort Zone

● ●

The Plank Across the Room

Here's an interesting proposition. Say I placed a wooden plank on the floor in a large room that's 12-inches wide and 20-feet long, and told you that I will give you $20 if you walk from one end to the other. You would instantly take up the challenge and easily win the $20. However, what if I raised the plank 500 feet off the ground and upped the offer to $1,000? You would probably exclaim "No way!" and walk away.

The plank's width remained the same. Your ability to physically walk across the plank hasn't changed. So why wouldn't you even attempt to walk across the plank for $1,000?

The reason lies in what is called your *comfort zone*. When you are standing on one end of the plank and picturing your death from falling 500 feet, your brain demands that you stay "right where you are." That is, it demands that you stay within your comfort zone.

Let's imagine that during the summer you like the temperature in your house to remain at 65 degrees. This can be done through a thermostat. However, let's imagine that in an effort to save some money, you install a rather shoddy thermostat that immediately turns the air conditioning on when the temperature reaches *anything* over *65*, and turns the heater on immediately when the temperature dips below *65*. Your energy bill would be quite high as the air conditioner and heater would be continually shutting on and off. Temperature control specialists therefore build into their thermostat a "comfort zone" where the air conditioning does not switch on until the temperature reaches two or three degrees above 65, and the heater does not turn on until the temperature decreases by two or three degrees below 65. Technically, this 4 to 6-degree margin is called a comfort zone. The mind also has a comfort zone—your self-image.

As we have already learned, your self-image is simply how you see yourself—how athletic you are, how smart you are, how comfortable with people you are, or how much money you believe you should make. All of these are not exact; they work within a zone. You may be an excellent bowler and a lousy first-baseman; you may feel very comfortable with written English but a real "bonehead" when faced with a lot of numbers, or, you may feel very comfortable in a room with people you know, but very awkward and self-conscious in a room full of strangers. As long as you stay within your comfort zone, however, you will behave the way you know you are.

When you find yourself out of that zone, most people become uncomfortable, or anxious, or self-conscious, not unlike walking into the wrong public bathroom (especially if it is already occupied!). When this happens, you instantly feel tension, and your creative subconscious protests, "You don't belong here. Get out of there as quick as you can!" The reason is because *all* of us seek emotional and psychological safety. We want to go back to the familiar, back to where we feel comfortable, even if that place of comfort is very unhealthy for us.

A plastic surgeon named Maxwell Maltz discovered this in the 1950s. He found that even after significant facial reconstruction, his patients *could not discern* any changes in their appearance as they looked at themselves in the mirror, no matter how significant the changes were! After studying and observing the psychology of his patients, he proposed that *any* change we make in our lives, including financial, spiritual, or physical, takes us out of our comfort zone, and actually sends a chemical signal to our entire body. Our brain picks up on this and we become very uncomfortable with the changes, whether they are good for us or not.

Dr. Maltz went on to become the founder of Psycho-Cybernetics, and in 1960 published *Psycho-Cybernetics, a New Way to Get More Living Out of Life*. Dr. Maltz introduced the principle that a person must have an accurate and positive view of one's self before setting goals, otherwise he or she will get stuck in a continuing pattern of limiting beliefs. He believed the self-image is the cornerstone of all the changes that take place in a person. If one's self-image is unhealthy, or faulty, all of his or her efforts will end in failure.

Our need to remain in our comfort zones is the reason that 80 percent of the teachers and staff at a career college where I taught were former students. They repeatedly told me that after graduating and experiencing the "real" world, they immediately returned to work at the college because it felt so comfortable there.

You've probably heard the advertisement: Join the Army and see the world. They don't! Our soldiers stationed in Germany or France seldom leave the base, and when they *do* leave, they head for the nearest McDonald's before returning as quickly as possible back to the base.

In addition, once you leave your comfort zone, your body actually physically reacts. The muscles in your upper body start to constrict, causing you to feel tense or uptight. Your stomach secretes more digestive juices, making you feel sick to your stomach. And, if you are attached to a lie detector and you deviate from the truth, perspiration instantly comes to your skin and you short the machine out.

Psychologically, the creative subconscious is again simply doing its job. Just as it makes sure that what you do lines up with your self-image, it also makes sure that you stay within your comfort zone. And as we have already learned, its tactics can be very devious. Has your self-talk included any of these phrases?

"I don't really belong here because I feel so out-of-place!"
"These aren't really my kind of people!"
"Why in the world am I taking the time to learn this anyway?"
"Why would I want to take that new position when I'm happy where I am!"

(Take caution with this last one. Perhaps there *is* no reason to take that new position. You must decide whether that is so, or you simply do not want to leave your comfort zone. More on that when we talk about goals in the next chapter.)

What also happens is that rather than saying, "Get out of here!" the creative subconscious simply finds fault with the new to go back to the old. "My kids need me. I don't have the money. It isn't the right time. But I haven't had pecan pie for such a long time!" The creative subconscious comes up with such wonderful reasons to not leave your comfort zone.

Just as changing your self-images can be difficult, changing your comfort zone can be just as challenging. However, rather than creating new self-images through affirmations, we must solve *this* new challenge by *expanding* our comfort zone. There are two ways to do this, one indirect, and one direct. Let's look at the indirect way first.

Expanding Your Comfort Zone through Creating Your Self-Images

It is helpful to realize that self-images actually fit within your comfort zone, as shown in Figure 1.

One definition of a person's comfort zone is simply a psychological area where he or she can comfortably function without feeling ill-at-ease or fearful. A definition of a person's self-image is a psychological picture, one of thousands, that shows how a person sees himself. That does not mean he likes them or that he would not like them changed, but that he has known them all his life and therefore feels the most comfortable with them.

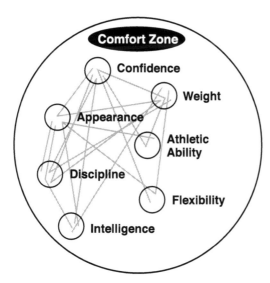

Figure 1

Here's a key point: When you create new self-images through affirmations, *your comfort zone must also be expanded!* For instance, let's imagine you want to create a self-image for yourself because you are so shy at parties. You therefore write an affirmation that says, "I am so comfortable with myself and others at parties, even with people I don't know." As you become more comfortable with people at parties, your comfort zone also grows to accommodate this new self-image. In other words, where you once avoided parties due to your shyness, your new self-image has caused your shyness and self-consciousness to significantly decrease. You therefore enjoy parties more, and your comfort zone has been expanded to include this new self-image (see Figure 2). To get you "over the hump" when attempting to expand your comfort zone, use visualization. Astronauts use flight simulators. Commercial airline pilots mentally picture the steps they would have to take if confronted with a flight emergency. A gymnast closes her eyes and pictures every step of her routine just before she starts it. This is what martial artists do with kung fu—practice in their mind to expand their comfort zones.

Since you are creating new self-images as the result of this book, your comfort zone is also expanding to make room for them, as shown in Figure 2.

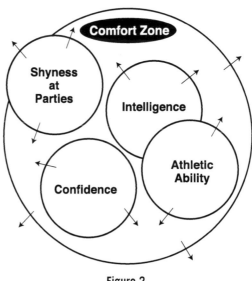

Figure 2

"The Next Time...I Intend to:" an Indirect Way of Expanding Your Comfort Zone

Actually, you have *already* learned the indirect way of expanding your comfort zone back in Chapter Twelve: By saying **"The Next Time...I Intend to."** Although it does not create new self-images as directly as affirmations do (which we will learn in Chapter Fifteen), it does contribute to seeing yourself differently. The potential behind this phrase is phenomenal. You are saying that the next time, you intend to expand your comfort zone by thinking differently and doing things differently.

You see, one reaction to shooting ourselves in the foot is immediately looking around to make sure that we are in still in our comfort zone. However, based on what we learned in the last chapter, we can react differently by following those three steps.

1. If necessary, make a mental note of your mistake and learn from it.
2. Feel *really* bad, but for no more than 15 seconds.
3. Finally, say: "**That is not like me anymore. The next time, I intend to...**" and create a picture in your mind of how you want to be the next time.

As we learned in Chapter Twelve, **The Next Time** has three encouraging inferences:

1. There will *always* be another Next Time.

There *are* no limits to the number of next times we have from now on. They never "run out." As long as we are alive, there is *always* another next time. Again, it is the mind-set great leaders take.

2. Always having a "Next Time" can be encouraging.

Each day can then be a "Do-over." Having another chance means there is *still* room for learning and growing and changing.

3. "The Next Time" is a far healthier reaction!

We will learn in the next chapter that without goals, people actually die. The Next Time can open you to new goals and reasons to grow and learn and change.

The Rubber Band Exercise

I use the following game with my students which I suggest you try. Acquire a loose rubber band that fits comfortably around your wrist. For the next 24-hours (and limit it to that), every time you say something negative about yourself, give the rubber band a little snap. This includes "How could I have been so stupid?" or "What's the matter with me?" or "Won't I ever learn?"

I once had a student call me in the middle of the night (my number was in the phone book) to ask if she could take the rubber band off, because her wrist was so sore from so many snaps! Another student stood in front of me the next day and told me how she felt *so* bad because she took the rubber band off to wash the dishes and forgot to put it back on. As she stood there, panic in her eyes, she pleaded, "What should I do now?!"

Do you see what we do to ourselves?

But don't stop with the snap!

When you *do* give yourself a snap, follow it with, **"That's not like me anymore The next time, I intend to..."** and tell yourself what you intend to do next time.

We *still* have so much to learn, and so many skills to add.

Next Chapter Preview

The next chapter prepares us for creating affirmations by helping us to understand why they work psychologically.

Remnants to Remember

- **Staying in your Comfort Zone**
    - Your self-images are not only how you see yourself, they also act as your comfort zone. As long as you behave the way you know you are, you are "within your comfort zone" and the brain is comfortable. However, when you begin to change, when you begin to develop new self-images that are overriding the old ones, your brain becomes very uncomfortable, and reacts accordingly. The reason is that all of us seek emotional and psychological safety. We want to go back to the familiar, back to where we feel comfortable, even if that place of comfort is very unhealthy for us.
- **"The Next Time...I Intend to"**—The Indirect Way of Expanding Your Comfort Zone
    - One quick-and-dirty way of expanding your comfort zone back is saying "The Next Time...I Intend to" when you make your next mistake.

Point to Ponder

1. Describe a time in your life when you did something that took you out of your comfort zone. How did your body react? Describe your feelings.

_____

_____

_____

_____

_____

_____

_____

_____

_____

CHAPTER FOURTEEN:
Our First Look at Affirmation

● ●

Men are disturbed, not by things, but by the view they take of them.
-Epictetus

A Deeper Look at Our Self-Talk

We have learned that "changing yourself" actually means *overriding* your self-images—the many ways you see yourself. However, not *all* your self-images need to be overridden. Some are just fine; others could use a little tune-up; some need **major** repairs; and if possible, some you would love to throw out.

We established in the Introduction to this book that your self-images are predominantly determined by what you tell you about yourself (i.e., your self-talk). We also discovered that your brain accepts anything you tell it about yourself without question. As I said in the Introduction, this can be a scary thought. However, based on what we have now learned together in the first 12 chapters, *we can use these facts to our advantage*. We'll discuss exactly how to do this throughout the rest of this book. First, though, let's take a deeper look at our self-talk.

Seeking the Strongest Picture

We have learned that your self-image is based on your self-talk, so to change your self-image, you must change your self-talk. Brain Principle #5 also tells us that what other people say about you impacts your self-talk (**You must agree with the opinion of another about you before it becomes a part of your self-image**). Therefore, one possible way of changing your self-image is to wait around for people to tell you how wonderful you are. But you know and I know that you won't live long enough for that to ever happen!

Perhaps another way would be to just keep telling *yourself* how wonderful you are. Maybe…if you do that over and over… you'll feel better about yourself. Well, if you have lived very long at all, you have already learned *that* doesn't work either!

Surprisingly enough, though, that kind of thinking does put us on the right track, based on a particular Brain Principle that we learned in Chapter Eight. That principle is **Brain Principle #10: Our brains seek the strongest picture.** In that chapter, we observed you learning how to ride a bicycle. When your father or mother warned you to NOT run into that rock 50 feet ahead, you kept your eyes fastened on that rock to make sure to avoid it. What happened? BAM! Right into the rock!

An affirmation is, in fact, that rock that you kept your eyes on. An affirmation is simply the stronger picture of a particular self-image than the one you have now. That stronger picture is then connected to change, goals and your future.

Change, Goals and Your Future

A goal, by its very nature, involves the future. An important element of changing yourself then, lies in the process of **bringing your future goals into your present**.

As you recall in Chapter Five, I would occasionally eat a pecan pie on a Saturday as a reward for being so disciplined with my eating and exercising the week before. I played that mental game for 25 years, and the weight *never* came off permanently. When I finally lost the extra weight, it did not come off because

I felt so bad about being so heavy that I worked hard enough to lose it. No, I first had to begin from the inside—with how I saw myself, with my self-image. In other words, the weight began coming off when I **brought a future goal into the present.** The future goal was, "I feel so great about myself and feel so light and eat so little because I weigh only 200 pounds" even though none of this was true at the time. However, over time this became the stronger picture. When I now sit down to eat and there is a pecan pie in front of me, I have very little desire to eat it. Why? Because my new self-image has *overridden* the old one of being a 230-pound man.

The statement, "I feel so great about myself and feel so light and eat so little because I weigh only 200 pounds" is called an *affirmation.* Affirmations aren't magical; they don't involve supernatural or "New Age" forces," or the "Power of Positive Thinking" forces. They are simply a statement declaring something to be true *whether it happens to be true at the moment, or not.*

Aren't I Simply Lying to Myself?

But isn't this just lying to myself? Good question! An affirmation is simply a statement you declare as true—to no one else but yourself, to, more specifically, your own mind. When created correctly (which we will learn how to do in the next chapter), an affirmation triggers a picture in your mind of a goal as if it has been *already accomplished.*

Although my affirmation was that of a 200-pound man, I did not become one for another two years. It *would* be a lie if I had told everybody that I was a 200-pound man for all those years. But I was not telling everyone else. I was simply saying this to my mind repeatedly as a belief *before* it happened, and as we have learned in the second Brain Principle: **The brain accepts what you tell it without argument.** So it is NOT a lie to my mind, for my mind accepts it as the truth.

An Important Note

As I said at the beginning of this chapter, you probably have some self-images that you would love to discard. Research shows, however, that other than by a pre-frontal lobotomy, you can't remove a self-image. Our self-images are wired in the neurons of our brain as patterns, just as our patterns of a city and a movie are stored (see Figure 1).

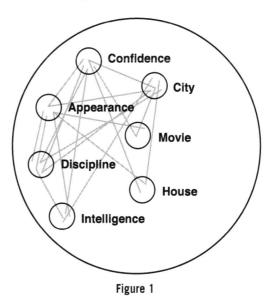

Figure 1

In my case, my self-image as a 200-pound man became the strongest picture. My old self-image of the 230-pound man has faded someplace in the recesses of my memory.

Words, Pictures, and Feelings

Before learning in the next chapter how to create affirmations, let's review one final element we must understand about how our brain works.

In the Introduction to this book, I said that while I am talking to you, you are talking to yourself three times faster. When I stop talking, you are talking to yourself six times faster. Some research suggests that although we usually speak out loud at the rate of 150 to 200 words per minute, we therefore talk privately to ourselves at the rate of approximately 1,300 words per minute.[75]

How is this possible?

The reason is because we think in words, pictures, and feelings, with the great majority in the form of pictures and feelings. For instance, when you think of a loved one, you do not picture them as a written description in a book. You see a picture of them in your mind's eye, accompanied by feelings. Since most of our thoughts take this form, we can then think of something in a fleeting moment that would take us many minutes of verbal speech to describe. Even one picture in our thoughts can be saturated with meaning that hundreds of verbal words would be required to explain.[76] Pictures thus become an extremely important part of affirmations, because in order for affirmations to work, they must become the stronger picture (remember **Brain Principle 10: Our brain seeks the strongest picture**).

Dr. David Bressler, head of the pain clinic at the University of California, Los Angeles (UCLA), works with people suffering from chronic pain. These people experience acute pain, some the results of injuries, others from unknown causes. One of Dr. Bressler's successful forms of therapy involves the use of visual images in the mind. In this process of mental imagery, Dr. Bressler has the patients visualize what the pain looks like. Once the patient has a visual image of the pain in mind, they work on changing the image of the pain (such as reducing its size and intensity). When doing so, in many cases, the actual pain also reduces in size and intensity.

In his own counseling practice, Dr. Stoop, whom we will meet later when we discuss the ABC's of emotions in Chapter Nineteen, works with many people with weight problems. One of the most important parts of the treatment is for the individuals to regularly practice creating a visual self-image of being thin. The degree of difficulty in ridding the body of excess weight is related to the difficulty they have creating that mental image of themselves 50 or 100 pounds thinner.[77]

It Doesn't Happen Overnight!

We also need to remind ourselves that long-term change, does *not* take place overnight. Returning to the example of teaching our children about the city in Chapter Two: Their brain needed time and reinforcement to lay down images and connect them together to form a pattern of a CITY. In the same way, your mind needs time and reinforcement to form new self-images.

Next Chapter Preview

There is one final principle that will further turn our brain into a motivator for change. In Chapter Six, we observed that after we do something stupid, we exclaim, "How could I have been so stupid?!" But we don't stop there! The conversation goes something like this: "How could I have been so stupid?! Well, that's not hard to answer. Don't you remember what you did last week? Oh, yeah, I remember that!" And on...and on...and on...

We then learned that the **brain is recording these memories and beliefs as if they were brand new—as if they had just happened!** So, when I say, "I feel so great about myself and feel so light and eat so little because I weigh only 200 pounds!" as an affirmation, the brain records that **as if it was brand new, as if it had just happened!**

In the next chapters, we begin learning exactly how the brain records what we tell it as if it has just happened.

Remnants to Remember

We learned three important points about goals and affirmations:

1. A goal, by its very nature, involves a future event that you want to happen in your life. However, we are taking the formation of goals a step further by emphasizing the fact that through affirmations, we will be bringing **your future goals into your present**...now!

2. Isn't that simply lying to myself? We answered that question by observing that an affirmation is simply a statement you declare as true—to no one else but yourself. When created correctly, an affirmation triggers a picture in your mind of a goal as if it has been *already accomplished.* If you knew with certainty that the goal would never be accomplished, *then* it would be a lie. But the whole purpose of your declaring an affirmation is that it *will* be accomplished, and sooner rather than later.

3. The reason we are able to process information far faster than we are able to listen or express it, is because we think in words, pictures, and feelings, with the great majority in the form of pictures and feelings. In fact, most of our thoughts take this form. This fact is extremely important to understand, because in order for affirmations to work, they must become the stronger picture.

Point to Ponder

1. We have learned that we do not have one self-image, we have thousands. The purpose of this book then, is not to change your self-image, but to change your self-images, and not all of them...just a few...the few that *you* want to change. We will be learning the first steps to do this in the next chapter. To develop the correct mind-set for this, however, simply write down a brief description of three or four self-images you have of yourself that you would like to change.

_____

_____

_____

_____

_____

_____

_____

_____

CHAPTER FIFTEEN:
How to Create an Affirmatio

• •

Reading this book has begun an endeavor in your life to reach a peaceful valley that lies on the other side of a tall mountain. Congratulations! You've just reached the top of the mountain! After reading and understanding the contents of *this* chapter, your remaining trek into the valley will be downhill and easier. You must simply stay on the path and learn as you walk.

Since we are at the top, let's stay here a while and learn how to write and practice writing affirmations. You will then be equipped to complete your journey and truly enjoy the benefits of the valley for the rest of your life.

As we have already learned, an affirmation is simply a 'trigger' to a picture you have created of a change already accomplished, even though it is not. This is how successful people think. They paint for themselves a picture of how they want to be. That picture is so strong and vivid that their brain naturally follows it. The mind *must* follow it, for as we have learned, its very nature is **to follow the strongest picture.**

Creating affirmations involves **12 Affirmation Guidelines**.[78] Let's look at each one now.

Sample Affirmation

1. I truly enjoy my life and relationships with other people.

2. I am so glad that I have excellent memory that enables me to recall people's names so easily.

3. I enjoy arriving at work on time because I love getting up in the morning.

1. They must be written and easily visible

Remember, the brain does not like change and will fight you tooth-and-nail to prevent these affirmations from changing anything. And it has quite an arsenal to do this, primarily with procrastination and laziness.

Of the many reasons for low self-esteem, *procrastination* is usually at the top or close to the top of the list. When you are procrastinating, how do you feel about yourself? It is also one of your mind's favorite weapons to combat change. Its approach is very subtle, and sounds something like, "Oh, you can write them down tomorrow. You'll be more rested and have clearer thinking."

As you know, this particular type of "tomorrow" somehow never materializes, and by the time it *does*, you have already forgotten what you were supposed to do. "Oh, yeah, I was going to write my affirmations today. But I'm so tired and have more important things to do. I'll do it tomorrow."

The mind also uses laziness to combat change. I often hear my students say, "Why do I have to write my affirmations down? Can't I just memorize them?" To answer that, I return to how we learn with images and patterns, as shown in Figure 1. As you remember, in order for the images to become a part of your Long Term Memory, they must be connected to other images, and this takes time, persistence, and repetition.

Write Them Down!

If you do not write down your affirmations, they will become fuzzier, and will never become a part of your long-term memory. Why not? By not taking the time to write them down, your brain will regard them as unimportant! In addition, if they are not written, they will either be forgotten, or eventually change so much in your mind that they become meaningless.

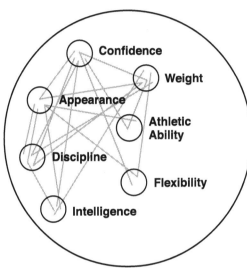

Figure 1

Keep Them Easily Visible

Even though an affirmation *is* written, placing it some place where you won't *automatically* see it daily will not change anything. Like the self-images in Figure 1, it must be reinforced every day over time until it becomes a picture of a new self-image that is stronger than the one you have now.

For my affirmations, I print out two sets. One I tape to the back of the door to our bathroom medicine cabinet where I shave each morning. When I open the door each morning, there they are. I then use the process we will learn in the next chapter to make these affirmations the stronger picture each morning. I have also placed them on the cover of my pocket calendar where I see them periodically throughout the day.

2. Make them personal

There are two reasons for this: One, these are *your* changes, not the changes that someone else thinks you should make, and two, your brain must have a vivid mental picture of how *you* will look. Only you can do that. An affirmation is successful only when the change is a change *you* want. Therefore, affirmations must *always* include the words "I" or "me."

3. Make them positive

This one is *so* important. Affirmations must say what you *want*, NOT what you don't want. "I will no longer smoke" is NOT an affirmation. It is simply another form of the "Shoulds" and the brain reacts by saying, "Yeah, you should. You just won't!"

This is because of the way our brains are wired. An incident in Galveston, Texas illustrates this point so well. Just before opening a new luxurious hotel next to Galveston Bay, the hotel manager took a last-minute tour of the rooms on the upper floors with his assistants. As they went from room to room, he expressed a concern. "Do you know what will happen? People with fishing gear will fish off the balconies, and the fishing weights will break the glass doors in the balconies below."

"Good point!" they all agreed. "What can we do?"

"I know!" exclaimed one assistant. "Let's place signs in each of the upper rooms." So in each of the rooms on the second floor and above, a sign was secured on each balcony glass door reading, **"Absolutely no fishing from the balcony!"**

You already know what happened. Right! Within the first week, four glass windows had been shattered.

"What shall we do?" groaned the manager. "Take down the stupid signs," suggested another assistant.

They did, and have not had a broken window since.

When you tell yourself what NOT to do, your attention is to automatically do it.

So: *No* negatives in your affirmations. No Shoulds! No Will Not's, and No Ought To's.

4. Always in the present tense

Affirmations must be written as if they are happening right now. If you keep them in the future, the brain figuratively relaxes. Why? Because it has been relieved from having to change. Nothing must change in the present if your affirmations are always in the future.

When you say, "I *will* lose weight," or "I will quit smoking," or "I will control my temper," the brain says, "Yeah. But we never live in the future do we, so I don't have to change anything!"

5. Indicate achievement

Clarity and accomplishments are so important in affirmations. "I am losing weight" could mean one pound or 100, and if the brain doesn't know, it will not know how to motivate you to achieve it. Rather: "It is great to feel so light because I eat and exercise like a 140-pound woman."

6. No comparisons

Affirmations are not a contest with someone else. They are not even a contest with yourself! An affirmation is simply a future picture of the way you want to be which you are bringing into your present. So, no comparisons!

7. Use action words

One of the keys to successful affirmations is their clarity. In other words, they need to trigger such strong pictures that your brain follows them naturally. Much of this is accomplished through *action* words, for they trigger the picture that you want as part of your life, and part of who you are. These words must vividly describe specifically the kind of behavior, the kind of job, or the kind of social world that you want. So, an affirmation that simply reads, "I get to work on time" will do no good because it provides no vibrant picture for the brain to follow. However, an affirmation which contains such action words as, "I *love* arriving to work early and *ready to excel*" provides a picture which your brain will then fasten onto.

8. Use emotion words

"I don't get angry," "I weigh 200 pounds," "I am at work on time," "I speak well in front of people," are statements, not pictures. The only reaction from your brain will be a yawn. Again, the key to a successful affirmation is a **stronger picture** in your mind's eye for the brain to follow. Successful affirmations are so vivid, so exciting, and so inspirational that your brain can't wait for them to happen. (More on this when we study goals in Chapter 17.)

9. They must be accurate

Remember that the brain looks for escape routes. One of its favorites is an affirmation that is so general, vague, unspecific, and fuzzy that it can't understand what you want. It therefore doesn't need to change anything. How early do you want to get to work? How much money do you want to make next month or next year? How many pounds do you want to lose, and when?

10. Keep them balanced

Affirmations can be written for all areas of your life. The Balance Wheel which we will be using at the end this chapter will help.

11. They must be realistic

It is deceptively simple to determine if your affirmations are realistic. If you can visualize them as actually happening, they are realistic. (More on this in Chapter 17.)

12. Keep them confidentia

Keep them confidential. These are YOUR affirmations. They are not a group project, or a team effort. No one needs to know about them except you.

Now that you know how to create effective affirmations, let's take some time to practice beginning on the next page.

Your Balance Wheel

A Balance Wheel helps you visualize the various areas of your life, and their relative importance to you right now. At the end of each spoke, write one or two words that express an area of your life that's important to you. These might include personal, spiritual, marriage, family, social, educational, health/physical, career/vocational/job, recreational/leisure time, health/mental, retirement, financial, community services.[79] If needed, draw some additional spokes (or, don't use them all). Then draw a dot between the end of the spoke and the middle indicating their importance to you, with the least important in the middle. Finally, draw a line from one dot on a spoke to the next. You will end up with a very weird looking closed jagged circle of lines. You now have a visualization that will help you narrow down those areas that are most important to you where you can create your affirmations.

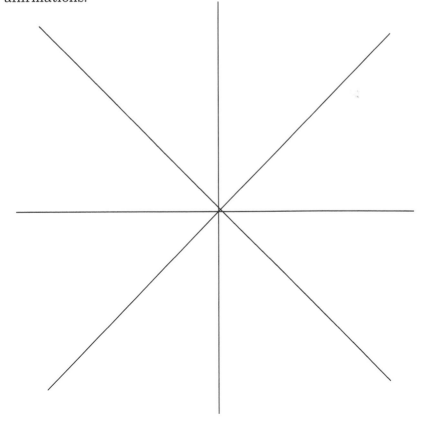

Effective sample affirmation

1. I like and highly respect myself because I understand college math so easily.

2. I love meeting new people I don't know at a party because I am as interesting to talk to as they are.

3. I love learning the Internet because it is such a vast source of knowledge.

4. I have an excellent memory. I easily remember the names of people I meet.

5. I love reviewing my affirmations daily because I see the changes in my life that are taking place.

6. I am so excited because I am selling so many products in my job and am making $60,000 this year.

7. I feel so great weighing so little because I eat and exercise like a 180-pound man.

8. I have a great deal of pride in my ability to find affordable and dependable residential care for my father.

9. I am so calm and at ease in stressful situations.

10. I am so comfortable making presentations in front of others because my presentations are so interesting.

11. I am so comfortable with myself when I meet new people.

12. Because of the patience and quiet support I give my son, he is learning how to love and respect me.

13. Because I am so valuable, I am financially responsible with my money.

14. Learning algebra is so easy for me because I enjoy treating it like a puzzle to be solved.

15. I love being my age because I have so much to contribute to those around me.

Ineffective sample affirmation
(The bolded words take away the power of an affirmatio .)

1. I like and highly respect myself because I **will** understand college math so easily. (**It must be in the present tense.**)

2. **I'll someday** love meeting new people I don't know at a party because **I will become** as interesting to talk to as they are. (**Again, must be in the present tense.**)

3. **I am learning the Internet because it has a lot of knowledge. (This is simply a statement. Your affirmation needs emotion and action words to make it a stronger picture.)**

4. I **would like to have** an excellent memory that easily remembers the names of people I meet. (**Wouldn't we all, but this is not an affirmatio .**)

5. I **should** review my affirmations daily to see the changes in my life that are taking place. (**No shoulds!**)

6. I **am trying really hard** to sell enough products in my job to make $60,000 this year. (**As we learned, "trying" is a meaningless term.**)

7. I **would feel** so great if I weighed so little because I ate and exercised like a 180-pound man. (**Again, this is a statement, not an affirmatio .**)

8. I **need to have** a great deal of pride in my ability to find affordable and dependable residential care for my father. (**Another statement!**)

9. I **will someday** be more calm and at ease in stressful situations. (**You brain says, "Whew! This takes me off the hook because the "will someday" is in the future, and I can only change the present."**)

10. I **would like to become** more comfortable making presentations in front of others because my presentations are so interesting. (**Wouldn't we all! But this will bring no change.**)

Next Chapter Preview

If you are older than 10, you have already learned that a simple set of "How-To's" accompanied by exercises are never enough for personal change. We have learned that as magnificent as our brain is, it does not like change. In addition, under any kind of stress, the loudest signals your brain sends are about what is happening *right at this moment* and how to survive it. Anything that's not immediately critical—such as changing yourself—gets drowned out.[80] Thus the remainder of this book is dedicated to the ways to teach your mind how to become your greatest motivator for change.

Points to Ponder

Your Own Affirmation

Now it is your turn. Based on the results of your Balance Wheel, choose three to six areas you would like to change. In the space below, first briefly describe the "Present Reality" followed by the Future Change you want to make in your life. Then write an affirmation to bring that change about.

Then write an affirmation to bring that change about using guidelines you learned in this chapter. They are:

- Write them down
- Keep them easily visible
- Make them personal
- Make them positive
- Keep them in the present tense
- Indicate achievement
- Make no comparisons
- Use action words
- Use emotion words
- They must be accurate
- Keep them balanced
- They must be realistic
- Keep them confidential

Present Reality

_____

_____

Future Change

_____

_____

Affirmatio

_____

_____

_____

_____

Present Reality

_____

_____

Future Change

_____

_____

Affirmatio

_____

_____

_____

_____

Present Reality

_____

_____

Future Change

_____

_____

Affirmatio

_____

_____

_____

_____

Present Reality

_____

_____

Future Change

_____

_____

Affirmatio

_____

_____

_____

_____

Present Reality

_____

_____

Future Change

_____

_____

Affirmatio

_____

_____

_____

_____

Present Reality

_____

_____

Future Change

_____

_____

Affirmatio

_____

_____

_____

_____

CHAPTER SIXTEEN:

The Proactive Power of Affirmation

. . . .

Having finished the previous chapter, with your affirmations in hand, you are now on your way down the other side of the mountain. Though there are more exciting principles we will be learning, we must first understand why your brain will do everything it can to prevent those affirmations from coming about. (We are doing this now so you won't be too surprised when some of your self-images do not change quite as quickly as you would like.) I'm reminded of Don Corleone's admonishment to his son in the movie *The Godfather:* "Keep your friends close, but your enemies closer."

Is our brain our enemy? Absolutely not! But we must teach it more than just adopting to change (it already *knows* how to do that, albeit grudgingly at times). Starting with this chapter, we will be looking at how to make it our greatest motivator.

The Boat Allegory

I do not fish because if I even *look* at a glass of water, I immediately become seasick. However, since drifting in a lake on a boat makes an excellent allegory for explaining the next step in making your affirmations real in your life, I thought this little tidbit would be a good way of starting this section. Imagine yourself in a small boat enjoying a sunny afternoon of fishing, with your automatic pilot causing your boat to drift in a northerly direction. After an hour of minimal results, you decide to steer the boat east where there might be more fish. So you arouse yourself from the back of the boat, take the steering wheel, turn the boat to the east and then let go of it…without adjusting the automatic pilot.

You already know what will happen.

As soon as you take your hands off the steering wheel, the automatic pilot takes over again and your boat drifts back to its original course. In other words, the automatic pilot prevents this change in direction from taking place.

In the same way, how you behave and how you think is governed by an automatic pilot—the self-images you have had all your life. They do not handle change lightly. In fact, as we learned in Chapter 13, other than by a pre-frontal lobotomy, your old self-images cannot be removed or 're-wired,' they must be over-ridden with stronger pictures.

So even with our affirmations, we still need to bring our mind over to *our* side, so that our affirmations bring about *long-term and permanent* changes in our lives.

Let's first look at what works…and what does not.

What Works, What Doesn't, and the Missing Ingredients

A cursory look at the books about our minds will reveal that many others have developed the same conclusions about the relationship between the brain and change. There are also a whole world of speakers and authors who have done exhaustive studies and conducted a LOT of inspirational workshops and written a *lot* of books.

However, as I observed in Chapter Four, **"Inspiration does *not* produce change!"** If there are so many "Solutions for Success" then, why are so many not creating *permanent* changes in our lives? And what then *is* the thread that runs through these "Solutions for Success" that actually *do* work over the long run?

There are in fact *three* threads, and thankfully we *have* addressed all of them. They are outlined in Shad Helmstetter's book, *What To Say When You Talk to Your Self.* I am paraphrasing what he says here:[81]

1. **True change must take place on the inside...in your mind.**

   As we will discover, without constant attention and effort, even the most exciting "Success Breakthroughs" run their course and eventually end up on our list of "good ideas" and "good intentions."

2. **True change must be based on how the brain actually works.**

   Without an understanding of how the human brain learns, and in turn, responds, directs, and controls us, it would be difficult (if not impossible) to create a success plan that works and keeps working indefinitely.

3. **A new word-for-word set of directions must be given to the subconscious mind.**

   These are the affirmations you have in your hand.

A Quick Note on The Power of Positive Thinking

My students often ask, "Isn't this just another version of the power of positive thinking?"

Not quite.

Although what we have been learning *is* a very close cousin, positive thinking does not go quite far enough to bring about lasting change; and "not quite far enough" is the difference between jumping all the way across a very deep chasm and jumping "not quite far enough."

Briefly, positive thinking claims that by deciding to think positively for the rest of your life, you will change your outlook on life, and, as a result, life itself. However, it ignores the thousands of self-images you have been living with all your life, many of which are *not* so positive. And as you already know (for *you* know them better than I), they seem to rear their ugly little heads when you run into those difficult or annoying circumstances that trigger them. This is why the decision to simply become a positive thinker is short-lived. In order for it *to* work, the negative self-images must be overridden with positive ones.

That is what you are learning how to do.

Those who have used affirmations before have also learned that they will not change anything by simply repeating them over and over. Let me say that again: **Affirmations will not change anything in your life by simple repetition.** You must create a stronger picture of yourself in your mind than the one you have now.

How? Let me now introduce a formula that holds a key to making affirmations work. The formula is:

I x V = R (I = Imagination, V = Vividness, and R = Reality)

As we looked at the Twelve Guidelines for Affirmations in the previous chapter, we saw that two of them were "Use Action Words" and "Use Emotion Words." These two are *so* important because they help create those vivid pictures we need to change our self-image. In turn, these new pictures need to be not only vivid, but as exciting as a child becomes when he sees his presents under the tree on Christmas morning. He can hardly wait to open them!

In the same way, you can hardly wait to begin seeing the new changes in your life that your affirmations are bringing about! And when that **vivid** and clear picture is repeatedly coupled with the wonderful feelings that accompany the changes taking place in your life, your creative subconscious treats that picture as a new **reality**.

The reason it does this is based on how our beliefs are formed.

How Our Beliefs Are Formed

Let's imagine an impressionable four-year-old boy who is far more interested in drawing dinosaurs than the thought of someday going to school. One morning he spends a whole hour drawing the most amazing tyrannosaurus rex he has ever drawn, and shows it to his big brother. His brother looks at it, and says, "That *looks stupid! You* can't draw!"

Now, his brother has expressed two opinions: The drawing looks stupid, and "You can't draw!" We learned from Brain Principle Five that **You must agree with the opinion of another**

about you before it becomes a part of your self-image. So this impressionable four-year-old brain takes the opinion "You can't draw!" and records it as an image (see Figure 1). After all, his oldest brother *is* the authority since he has *his* drawings on the refrigerator. The little boy returns to his room, creates an even more intricate stegosaurus, and shows it to his older sister. She has some of her friends in her room at the time and doesn't want her little brother hanging around, so she haphazardly expresses the same opinion. Again, his brain records a second image of her opinion that "You can't draw." (See Figure 1 again.) He finally decides that since his mother is the *ultimate* authority, he will draw a "Super Triceratops" for her...on the wall of his room. After it's finished, he runs to the kitchen, grabs her skirt, drags her to his room, and opens the door in triumph. Her reaction is not what he expected. A third image is recorded. "You...can't... draw!" (Again, Figure 1.)

The Fourth Element

A fourth element however, is far more damaging than the other three put together. It is represented in Figure 1 by the circle marked "**Myself—I Can't Draw.**" As we have already learned, our brain not only records what others tell us, **it records what we tell ourselves**. So if this little boy accepts what others told him, he will begin telling himself the same, but this time over-and-over, and each time he says it, the brain records it as a new image. Can you see how we are affected by what we tell ourselves?

Now let's fast-forward to the boy's first day of kindergarten. After snack time, Mrs. Sikes stands before the class and exclaims, "Children, we're going to do something very special on our first day. We are going to get out the crayons and construction paper and then we are going to draw!" The little boy, sitting cross-legged on his mat, says to himself, "In your dreams!" Why? Because his brain has created a very clear belief: "I Can't Draw!"

This is in fact how *all* of our beliefs are formed about ourselves; we were not born with them. These beliefs then are based on two elements: 1.) The responses, comments and reactions of other people, and 2.) What we say to ourselves about ourselves. Both of these accumulate to become our beliefs, and these beliefs about ourselves in turn form our self-images.

The Proactive Power of Affirmation

Our self-images then are based on our beliefs. These beliefs are in turn based on both the reactions and opinions of others, and the reactions and opinions of ourselves. Is there a way to

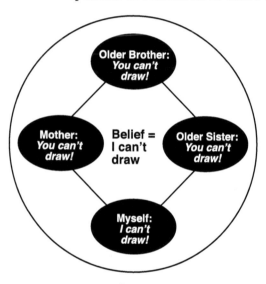

Figure 1

change these beliefs? Yes—through the *proactive* power of affirmations.

The meaning behind the word 'proactive' is "acting in advance." An affirmation does just that. Rather than waiting for *others* to form our self-images by telling us who they think we are and what we can do, affirmations enable us to create our *own* self-images *in advance* (proactively). In other words, we no longer need to wait on what others tell us about how well we can or cannot draw, or how heavy or light we are, or how well we can or cannot do math. We can make these changes ourselves by *proactively* creating our own self-images. You need not wait for anyone, and you do this by developing the habit of imprinting your affirmations.

How Are Habits Formed?

So how do you teach your mind a new habit? This is important to understand for three reasons:

1. Creating new self-images requires imprinting new affirmations consistently, every day. In other words, imprinting your affirmations *must* become a habit in order for any real change to take place.
2. Understanding how habits are formed can give you the tools to form them.
3. Understanding how your brain forms habits also helps you know what to expect psychologically as they are being formed.

We discovered in Chapter Two how we learn. Using a city as an example, we saw how our brain lays down images (such as my reading a book about the city), and connects those images to other images through neural connections. As more and more images are laid down, more and more become connected to one another. Each neural connection involves a nerve cell containing a central processing headquarters and a long sending fiber (or *axon*) over which it relays messages. Nerve cells also have lots of tiny receiving fibers (or *dendrites*) for incoming messages (see Figure 2).

Frequently used dendrites form tiny bumps called "boutons," from the French word for buttons. The more boutons a nerve cell has, the more easily and quickly it's able to make connections to other nerve cells. It is almost as if the repetition wears a groove in the brain in the

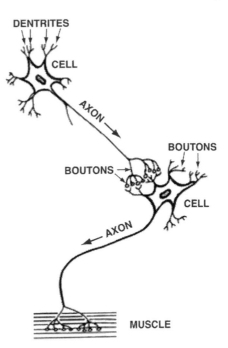

Figure 2

same way a mountain trail is created by repeatedly walking over the same path.

You Are Not *Replacing* Your Self-Images

We saw in Chapter Six that our beliefs about ourselves (i.e., our self-images) are learned the same way we learn about a city. Boutons, unfortunately, do not go away when they are no longer used anymore than self-images are somehow deleted from our brain. And because the old pathways are still there, the chance of falling back into a bad habit is always present, as when an alcoholic "falls off the wagon." However, by learning how to repeatedly imprint your affirmations, as we learn in the next chapter, new self-images become stronger than the old. Over time, more boutons are created on the new pathway than on the old one, and the "path" will wear deeper. As it becomes easier to take the new route, the new self-image is being established.

How Long Does This Take?

The time it takes for new habits to be formed is the same as the time it takes for patterns to be formed. A good approximation can be found by looking at two scientific studies, one from a plastic surgeon in the 1950s, and one from the National Aeronautics and Space Administration (NASA).

Dr. Maxwell Maltz (the same Dr. Maltz we met in Chapter Thirteen who founded Psycho-Cybernetics) also discovered that it took approximately 21 days for amputees to cease feeling phantom sensations in their amputated limb. This prompted Dr. Maxwell to work with his clients' self-image *prior* to surgery, and he discovered that he could assist them to acquire an improved self image without surgery, using the same 21-day period to create changes in their mindset, and that surgery then became unnecessary for them. He was then able to expand these observations to habits in general, and the '21 Day Habit Theory' has become an accepted part of programs helping people both break and create new habits.

The second set of studies took place at NASA, the National Aeronautics and Space Administration. To test the impact of being in space for long periods of time, NASA developed a set of goggles which flipped everything that was seen by 180 degrees. You therefore saw the top of your vision on the bottom, and the bottom on the top. These goggles were then fitted to a number of astronauts to test their ability to function with their world looking topsy-turvy. After wearing these goggles 24 hours-a-day for 26 days without ever taking them off, something very interesting happened. Their vision turned right-side up again, and they were able to see everything as normal, even with the goggles on. The goggles had not overridden what they saw, their brains had.

What had they done? They had created the neural connections that we explored in the second chapter when we discovered how our brain learns about a CITY. Their brains laid down these same neural connections. This is how our brains rewire themselves to form habits. There are, however, two barriers that must be understood and overcome if real change is take place in your life. Both of these have to do with goals; one is the *structure* of your goals, and the other is the *incentive*. Let's look at the first in the next chapter, and the second in the chapter which follows it.

Next Chapter Preview

The affirmations you have created are simply goals that you have personalized and visualized for yourself. In the next chapter, we will see how important goals really are.

Remnants to Remember

- The three requisites for successful change:
    1. True change must take place on the inside...in your mind
    2. True change must be based on how the brain actually works.
    3. A new word-for-word set of directions must be given to the subconscious mind.
- Imagination x Vividness = Reality (I x V = R)
    - You must create a stronger picture of yourself in your mind than the one you have now.
- The Proactive Power of Affirmations
    - 'Proactive' simply means "acting in advance," and an affirmation does just that. Rather than waiting for others to form our self-images, affirmations enable us to create our own self-images in advance...proactively.

Points to Ponder

1. Describe a time in your life when you set a goal for yourself and, like the allegory of fishing on the lake, the goal floated away when you let go of the steering wheel.

---

2. Can you think of a specific habit you formed? How did it become permanent in your life, and how long did it take to form?

CHAPTER SEVENTEEN:
Making Your Mind Your Motivator: Part I

• •

Creating Goals that Work

Why Spend More Time On Goals?

You have now created your affirmations (which are simply your personal goals) in Chapter Fifteen. Why then are we spending even more time exploring goals? Haven't we already learned enough about them? No, we have not.

The reason is that even though we learned how to create goals, we must also know how to set them *effectively* so their structure is correct. This is the reason that most goals are never met. Like most other skills we have, the skill of goal setting must, for the most part, be learned.

Think about this: Most of us periodically have had goals throughout our lives. These goals, however, have often been vague, confusing, conflicting, unchallenging, impossible, meaningless, or unrelated to our lives. Even more frustrating is how they do not usually bring about the real long-term changes we desire in our lives. However, those long-term changes are what you want. They are the reason you are reading this book...to learn how to *bring* permanent changes to your life.

So let's start with the importance of goals.

The Importance of Goals in Your Life

As we study the psychology of man, the more we see how important goals become in our lives. In fact, you probably don't have *any idea* as to their importance. Without goals in our lives, we die. Death actually occurs!

There have been many studies that verify this. One which is quite vivid came from the treatment which American Prisoners of War suffered during the Korean War. Their North Korean captors developed a way to take away from those prisoners any hope of ever being rescued, which also included any goals they might have had for their lives. When this happened, many of these young men would crawl into the corner of a cell, put a blanket over their head, and be dead in three days—without anyone ever touching them.

Dr. Viktor Emil Frankl was an Austrian neurologist, psychiatrist, and a Holocaust survivor. He was also the founder of logotherapy, and published *Man's Search for Meaning* which chronicled his experiences as a concentration camp inmate. He described how those inmates who had goals in their lives, even very sordid ones, were the ones who were most likely to survive the death camps. Those who gave up—who didn't have any goals—were the ones who often did not survive. He found that the key to surviving the camps was to find meaning in even the most trivial forms of existence.

Further evidence is found in a study[82] published in 2005 which indicated that men and women who retire early at age 55 have a significantly increased risk of death as compared with those who retire at 65. In this research, death was almost twice as likely in the first 10 years after retirement at age 55 compared with those who continued working. The study, published online by the *British Medical Journal*, was adjusted to take into consideration factors such as sex and socioeconomic status. Although some workers in the study retired at 55 because of failing health, "these results clearly show that early retirement is not associated with increased survival."

So if our goals are so important, why is it so hard to fulfill them? Let's explore that next.

You Are Working Against Your Subconscious

One of the significant traits of our humanness is our ability for ordinary *forethought*. Forethought is simply our imagination taken forward. We call it "ordinary" because we do it all the time. When we make a cake, our forethought imagines what the cake will look like and how it will taste. When we look at an "Exit" sign over a door, we imagine ourselves leaving the building when we walk through that door. When we see directional signs on the freeway, we imagine where we will be when we follow the directions of those signs.

The affirmations which you created at the end of Chapter Fifteen are simply a form of forethought that you have (hopefully) written down. However, in order for them to change you, they must take *you* forward to a place (or places) where you have never been before. Most of us do not set our affirmations to do this.

For example, affirmations such as, "I will walk three miles every other day!" or "I will quit drinking!" or "I will arrive on time at work" all sound very inspirational, especially as New Year's resolutions. However, your brain disregards the **"I will's"** as readily as it disregards the **"I should's."** As we learned in Chapter Eight, when we say, "I should weigh less!" "I should be a non-smoker" or "I *should* be wealthy," your brain simply says, "Yeah! You're right! You should! YOU'RE JUST NOT!" The "should's" only recognize the problem and have no intention of changing it.

In the same way, when you say, "I *will* walk three miles every other day!" or "I *will* quit drinking!" your brain knows that the "I will's" always refer to the future, and since it does not live in the future, its response is the same: "Yeah! Maybe you will...but maybe you won't! How should I know? I won't be there! So I won't need to change." Again, the "I will's" do not give your mind any motivation for change.

When creating affirmations, you therefore need to remember that you are working against your own subconscious. Its job is to keep you in your comfort zone, to keep you the way you are, to *stop* you from changing! While your mind *can* become your greatest motivator for change, its *natural* impulse is to stop you from changing.

Believe it or not, the answer to solving this dilemma was found in a school of psychology over 150 years ago, called "Gestalt Psychology." Let's look at that now.

Closing the Gap

The word *Gestalt* is German for shape or figure. Gestalt originated in Berlin early in the 20th century as a theory of the mind and brain which observes that the brain has a self-organizing tendency which perceives the whole as different from the sum of its parts. More specifically, it refers to the brain's need for order in its universe. According to Gestalt, every human being is working to maintain that order in his or her mind.

To illustrate, look at Figure 1:

Figure 1

When you first look at this picture, all you see are black and white specks. But as you look at it further, the image of a Dalmatian sniffing the ground begins to form in your mind. In other words, what originated as black and white specks becomes a picture of a dog in the foreground, and the shade from a tree in the background. And the longer you look the clearer these images become. The whole becomes greater than its parts. That's Gestalt.

Figure 2 is even clearer.

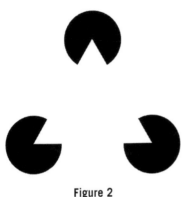

Figure 2

Can you see the triangle? Of course you can. But there is really is no triangle there: Simply three pack-men facing one another. However, if you look long enough, you can almost sense your brain *drawing* lines between the pack-men to create that triangle.

Figure 3 shows a third illustration of Gestalt.

Figure 3

Can you see the globe? Again, there really is no globe there, simply some black triangles spaced together. However, your mind takes those triangles and forms for itself the appearance of a globe. This is another example of the whole becoming more than the sum of its parts.

Figure 4

Now how does all of this relate to setting goals and affirmations? To answer that, imagine that you went to a friend's house and saw the picture of the Mona Lisa hanging on her living room wall, exactly as you see it in Figure 4. Now this picture is a perfect copy of the original. However, you immediately see it is tilted, which causes an almost obsessive urge to straighten it! In fact, if you sit down for dinner facing the picture, it would take a great deal of discipline to prevent yourself from running over to the living room wall to straighten the picture.

That's Gestalt: You need to straighten the picture, or as the followers of Gestalt psychology would say, you need to "bring order in your universe." Order simply means that you have an idea of what is right—how a piece of cake should taste, how a room should look, how a car should drive, how the Mona Lisa should hang on a wall, and how your life should look. If reality does not match your idea of what something should look like, your mind can become very anxious and tense.

This tension causes you to want to resolve the conflict: To fix the problem, to straighten the picture, to close the gap. This simply means that goal setting that really works *deliberately* causes a conflict; a conflict between your affirmations and how you are now. For instance, if you see yourself as a "C" student and keep getting "C" grades, there is no conflict. However, if you have created an affirmation that says, "I love being an A student in all the courses I am taking," there *will* be a conflict if you keep getting C's. Your mind therefore becomes your motivator for solving conflict. Let's see how.

Making Your Mind Your Motivator: Part I

A few pages back, we discovered that goals such as "I *will* walk three miles every other day!" or "I *will* quit smoking!" usually don't work. Your mind simply responds, "Sounds inspirational! Maybe you will...but maybe you won't! How should I know? I don't live in the future, and I have enough to think about just dealing with the present." The "I will's" and the "I should's" therefore do not give your mind any motivation for change.

Where does that motivation come from? It comes from the same place where you got the motivation to straighten the tilted picture of the Mona Lisa. The moment you saw that it was not the way it should be, you not only became anxious and tense, you had to hold yourself back from running over to straighten the picture. That energy which arose came from your mind's need to "close the gap" by fixing the problem, in this case, straightening the picture.

When you create enough of a gap between your affirmations and the way you are now, your mind will release the energy and creativity to close the gap automatically. You won't have to think about it, for that is the way your mind works. By making your affirmations far more vivid than the way you see yourself, they become a reality on the subconscious level, and then your mind works on making them a reality in your life.

Here's an exciting thought: You already have most of the tools to do that! Those are the affirmations you created in Chapter 15. Now let's learn the steps to imprint them so that they become a reality on the subconscious level.

The Steps for Imprinting Your Affirmations [83]

1. **Be sure that your one-sentence affirmations are written, and are someplace you see them automatically every day.**
2. **Review each affirmation daily...without fail.**
    To form a habit, they must be reviewed for at least 21 days, though 30 days is better.
3. **When reviewing your affirmations**, read them slowly, then close your eyes and visualize the image that these words trigger.

4. **Vividly picture them**. The picture you get by visualization is vitally important because it must become a stronger picture than the way you see yourself now. Just like the little boy fastens his eye on the rock in the road when learning how to ride a bicycle, your brain will fasten onto this new picture. Remember that the clearer the picture, the more effective it is. The picture in your mind should not be hazy: It should be specific, down to the finest details you can imagine. Clarity and detail are two qualities that we seek, so as you read the words, you imagine the event in vivid detail and see the accomplishment of your goal.

5. **Feel the emotion** as if the event is happening right now. You might try borrowing from a past positive experience and bring the good feeling into your present affirmation.

What Is Your Brain Doing?

When you follow these steps consistently, something very interesting happens neurologically. These repetitious thoughts move from neuron to neuron by leaping across the gaps, or synapses in between each neuron. These gaps are called "synaptic chasms." To cross each chasm, a certain electrical threshold must be reached and exceeded. These synaptic chasms are the location of the boutons shown back in Figure 2 in Chapter 16. The more boutons a synapse has, the more they lower these electrical thresholds, and connections can be made more easily and quickly. Over time, as you make these affirmations the stronger picture, it becomes easier and easier for them to travel from one neuron to the next. In a sense, you are bushwhacking a new pathway with your affirmations.

Neuroscientists have an expression: "Neurons that fire together...wire together."[84] As you repeat your affirmations, your neurons literally wire themselves together, forming the same patterns which we form as we learn about a city (as described in Chapter Two). In time, your new path becomes a superhighway, changing you from the inside out. You simply need to create your goals, your visions, your dreams...and by creating affirmations for each one and repeating them in the way I have just described, you will grow into them. That is how your mind is wired, and can become wired over and over.

But how does my brain know where to lay this superhighway? John Medina explains this so well in his book, *Brain Rules*.[85]

> "A keynote speaker at a university administrator's luncheon told of the story of the wiliest college president he ever encountered. The institute had completely redone its grounds in the summer, resplendent with fountains and beautifully manicured lawns. All that was needed was to install the sidewalks and walkways where the students could access the buildings. But there was no design for these paths. The construction workers were anxious to install them and wanted to know what the design would be, but the wily president refused to give any. He frowned, "These asphalt paths will be permanent. Install them next year, please. I will give you the plans then." Disgruntled but compliant, the construction workers waited.

> "The school year began, and the students were forced to walk on the grass to get to their classes. Very soon, defined trails started appearing all over campus, as well as large islands of beautiful green lawn. By the end of the year, the buildings were connected by paths in a surprisingly efficient manner. "Now," said the president to the contractors who waited all year, "you can install the permanent sidewalks and pathways. But you need no design. Simply fill in all the paths you see before you!" The initial design, created by the initial input, also became the permanent path."

Goal-Setting Has Nothing to Do With Time

In order for your affirmations to really work, you must understand another element: Goal-setting has *nothing* to do with time, it has to do with what you *want*. If your goal is to lose a certain number of pounds in a year, you lock out losing them sooner. Further, when you attach a time-element to a goal, your mind usually waits until the *very* last minute to get serious about fulfilling it, and then it is usually too late…and you give up. Remember, your mind does not like change, and it undermines you when it can.

What is the shortest time frame you can have for reaching a goal? A month? No! A week? No, keep going! A day? No. Now! Yes, *now!* When you write your affirmations, you write them as if they have *already* occurred *right now!* You have *already* paid off that loan, you have *already* lost that weight, you have *already* taken that trip to Alaska…now! But you haven't! So you have a problem. You have created a gap that needs to be closed. To close the gap, your mind becomes a driving force and motivator to fix the problem—such as straightening the picture.

Some goals may require two years, so go ahead and write down two years. For most affirmations and goals, however, writing them down as if they have already happened is what energizes you in unbelievable ways. Your mind truly becomes your strongest motivating force. The reason is because you are telling yourself that you have it, and you don't! You are telling yourself that you have lost the weight, and you have not. You are telling yourself that you no longer do this or that, and you are still doing it.

Beware of the How Question

Another element in goalsetting that deserves some caution is the "How" question. The How Question usually comes up when you share your goals with others. They then respond by fixing their eyes on you and ask, "Now *how* are you going to do that!?" You then feel a bit defensive and answer, "I really haven't thought that out yet." Their retort is then, "Well, that's just silly! That's unrealistic! That's impractical!" They then recommend that you ratchet your goals back to where you *know* how you are going to achieve them, right down to the very steps.

I have seen so many people map out their goals so fastidiously that, for the sake of "being realistic" they are never met.

You need to remember that when you have a vision or a dream or a goal, and you look at how far you are from it now, anxiety and tension immediately builds up. But when your goals become strong enough, your mind begins to *invent* ways to fulfill them! You need not know all the steps that must be taken to fulfill your goals, you simply need to know how to set them, and your mind will figure out many of the steps for you. That is how your mind works.

For example, just before graduating from high school, our daughter, Sarah, developed a passion to attend the University of San Francisco (USF). We sat down as a family and looked at the financial impact, which was ominous to say the least. However, we did not let the "How" question stop us from creating a goal for Sarah to attend USF. We simply set up some parameters (such as we are not going deeply in debt for her to attend, etc.).

The very next morning as I drove to work (using the same route I had been taking for seven years), I noticed a sign on the freeway for the University of San Francisco. I had never notice it before—a sign advertising a satellite campus right in my own backyard. The reason I now saw the sign was because USF was now important to me, and my mind had began searching for ways to fulfill our goal of Sarah going to USF. I made contacts with the staff at the satellite campus, and eventually began teaching at USF. I was given a free unit for every unit I taught. This alone paid for most of Sarah's education and most of my Masters in Information Systems.

The brain does indeed find a way. All *you* need to do is set the dream, set it correctly, and you will grow into it.

The "Realistic" Test

Wait a minute? Does avoiding the How Question mean that *any* goal you set is alright to have, no matter how 'expensive' or "unrealistic" or "far out" it may seem? By no means! So what is the balance? In other words, is there a way to know how realistic a goal really is?

Absolutely, and it can be tested very easily. The test is whether or not you can see *yourself* accomplishing that goal. If you can, then it's probably realistic. If not, then it's probably not. If your goal *is* so 'far out" you cannot see yourself attaining it, then it *is* time to reassess, and perhaps bring it back a bit.

Next Chapter Preview

One of the primary reasons that goals we set are not reached is because we have given them the wrong incentive. We will learn how to change that in the next chapter.

Remnants to Remember

- The Importance of Goals in Your Life
- You Are Working Against Your Subconscious
  - One of the significant traits of our humanness is our ability for ordinary forethought—which is simply our imagination taken forward.
- Closing the Gap
  - Our brain has an inordinate need for order in its universe, and to close any "gaps" we may have made. Its need to close these gaps can be used as an incentive to meet our goals.

Points to Ponder

1. Describe a time in your life when you set a goal for yourself and let the "How?" question get in the way.

CHAPTER EIGHTEEN:
Making Your Mind Your Motivator: Part II

• •

Changing the Have-To's to Get-To's

Look At Your Incentives

We concluded at the end of the last chapter that there are two barriers that must be understood and overcome for you to consistently meet your goals. The first was the *structure* of your goals. We learned that when your mind is given a clear and vivid picture of what you to want to be, it then creates the energy and creativity to override what you are now. To accomplish this, we write our affirmations as if they have *already* occurred...now! We have *already* paid off that loan, or we have *already* taken that trip to Alaska...now! The fact that we have not causes a tremendous mental gap which our mind endeavors to close.

Some of the ways the mind attempts to close this gap, however, can be rather devious. For example, rather than creating the energy and creativity to meet your goals, it first suggests that your goals are "unrealistic" or "foolish" or "too expensive." Other suggestions include your being "too old" or "too young" or "not smart enough" or "you don't have the money." One of its favorites is that you "pull back" and "wait for a better time." All of these suggestions are simply attempts your mind uses to keep you in your comfort zone, to keep you from changing. Don't be surprised by this—remember, this is the mind's job.

You *will* hear these suggestions, so don't be surprised when you do. However, you do need to counter them with some solid psychological principles that we will now explore. These principles involve a second barrier which your mind tries to erect to keep you from changing. This second barrier involves your *incentives* for reaching your goals, and they fall into two categories; *restrictive motivation* and *constructive motivation*. Let's look at the first.

Restrictive Motivation

We have all had the feeling of being forced into doing something we didn't want to do. We may have still done it, but we rebelled with every breath we took, and this alone took up a lot of our energy. This is interesting: If I had you hold up the palm of your hand, and I pushed against it with my own palm, you would immediately push back! Your mind reacts the same way, and it all has to do with motivation.

Let's first clarify what motivation is *not*. It is not some mysterious energy that is aroused after hearing a motivational speaker, or reading an inspiring article in a magazine. "Motivation" comes from the word "motive" which is simply whatever causes a person to act in a certain way, or do a certain thing. In the present context, it is the *reason* behind your goals.

Restrictive motivation is almost always based on fear, and usually ends with the words "or else." *Do this...or else* followed by a vivid description of what will happen if you don't. Unfortunately, most of us were raised on restrictive motivation—by our families, churches, schools or teachers. Most of us have raised our own children using restrictive motivation.

However, it is vitally important to understand that *restrictive* motivation acts as a death knell to most of our goals. I'll say this again: This type of motivation acts as a *death knell* to most of our goals. This happens due to the three ways we react to restrictive motivation: **Procrastination, slovenly work,** and **creative avoidance.** Let's look at each one briefly.

Procrastination

When you look at the various lists that name the reasons for low self-esteem, procrastination usually ranks close to the top, if not at the very top. The reason: How do you feel about yourself when you are procrastinating? Not good, right? Yet procrastination is usually our first reaction when someone tells us that we *have to* do something. We suddenly become very tired, or we find some reason to put it off. The psychological reason is that humans have a real sense of their own dignity—even if they do not always recognize it. When you feel you are being pushed or coerced against your will, your dignity is aroused, and your mind reacts by saying, "You are telling me that I have to, but if I have my *own* way, I would rather be doing this over here, or that over there." In other words, your mind suddenly finds a reason to put it off.

Slovenly Work

If you have ever told your teenagers that they *have to* wash the dishes, they will do them…but very grudgingly. And when they are through, they will have left the knives and forks…and pots and pans. After all, "You said to just do the dishes!" This is slovenly work—doing the job just barely enough to get by.

Creative Avoidance

Another more subtle ploy your teens might use when you tell them they *have to* wash the dishes is this: They suddenly remember a homework assignment is due no later than tomorrow, so they promise to do the dishes "later." Of course, they usually never do. Notice that when someone says that you *have to* do this job, all sorts of other jobs arise in your mind that must be done first. That is called creative avoidance.

All of this leads to the fact that **it makes no difference whether *I* am telling you must do something, or you are *telling yourself* you must do something, your brain often reacts in the same way: Through procrastination, slovenly work, or creative avoidance.** In other words, it makes no difference whether I am forcing you, or you are forcing yourself, your mind reacts the same way. When you tell yourself you *have to* do something, your mind will try to get out of it. This is the way your mind works.

This new principle is critical to understand as you are creating your affirmations, because the motivation *behind* the goals will largely determine how much your mind intends to help you reach them. And as we have just learned, goals based on *restrictive motivation* causes your mind to actually work *against* you.

Let's now look at another way to make your mind your *motivator* through *constructive motivation*.

Constructive Motivation

An understanding of constructive motivation must begin with the realization that there are very few have-to's in our lives. Most choices are based on free will. Since this statement usually causes an immediate protest in my class until we explore it, let's explore it now.

All of us *think* we have a lot of "have-to's in our lives. We have to get dressed; we have to brush our teeth; we have to pay our taxes; we have to change the diapers. However, none of these are really have-to's. We don't *have to* get dressed; or brush our teeth; or pay our taxes; or change the diapers.

What do I mean? Think of this:

- You don't really have to get dressed...if you can handle the stares, the embarrassment, and eventually the police dragging you away.
- You don't have to brush your teeth. Stop brushing them, and you won't have to deal with people being around you.
- You don't *have to* pay your taxes (though you'll probably end up in jail).
- You don't *have to* change the diapers; left on long enough, they'll eventually fall off.

When my students protest, "But I don't *want* to live that way!" I point out that along with free will, they **must also accept the consequences of those decisions.** (There is a second option which we'll consider at the end of this section.) In other words, if they decide to not get dressed, the consequences *will*

be stares, embarrassment, and the police. If they deci
brushing their teeth, the consequence will be extreme
breath and cavities. If they decide to stop paying their
consequence may be a new home in jail. And if they de ___ ⌄⌄ ₁₁⌄
longer change the diapers, the consequence will be a particularly
unpleasant odor emanating from their house. My point is that
there is only one real have-to in the world (although there *are* a
few more)—you have to die. Everything else is your choice. However, you must also accept the consequences of your decisions.

The realization that almost everything you do is a matter of
free choice opens a whole new dimension to goal-setting; a dimension that most of us have never known was available. I call
this dimension *constructive motivation.* Constructive motivation
is based on the *value* of what you *want* to do, rather than what
you *have to* do. It is a "get-to," rather than a have-to. You don't
have to accept the consequences of your decisions, you *welcome*
them. Your goals are then based on the following three incentives:

- **I don't have to meet them, I want to meet them.**
- **I like what I am becoming, and I love what I am doing.**
- **They are my idea.**

In order for your mind to become your motivator, these three
incentives must be behind all of your goals.

With these in mind, let's return to the four have-to's we considered before and convert them to get-to's:

- You don't have to get dressed, you get dressed because what you wear is a reflection of who you are, and you *like* who you are.
- You don't *have to* change the diapers, you *get to* because you can then enjoy those precious moments of that little face staring up at you while you are changing them. That time will be gone so quickly, so you intend to enjoy every moment while you can.
- You don't have to brush your teeth, you get to spend two minutes in the morning and two minutes in the evening in exchange for your teeth feeling squeaky clean all day, as well as them being cavity-free.
- And you *don't* have to pay your taxes…you want to pay your taxes because they enable you to live where you are living and do what you are doing.

Releasing the Energy

The primary reason constructive motivation can be so affective for goal-setting is the motivational energy your mind releases. When you are doing things you want to do, the energy just seems to come from nowhere. Let me give you a quick example: Have you ever had to force your children out of bed on Christmas morning? Did you have to go into their rooms and remind them that it is now time to unwrap the presents! Of course not! You can hardly keep them in bed after 6 a.m. Why? Because they are so energized to run into the living room and see the presents under the tree, followed by the joy of unwrapping them.

Here's another example. There is a pre-school boy who has an older brother who is already in kindergarten. The pre-school boy listens to all his brother's stories about school. The more he hears, the more excited the boy becomes. When the day finally arrives for *his* first day of school, you can hardly keep him at the breakfast table. Why? Because he *wants* to go to school; going to school has not yet become a *have-to*.

I have a friend who gets up at 3 a.m. every morning to run up a hill behind his house for an hour. He has been doing this for as long as I have known him. I remember sitting down for lunch with him and asking where he gets the discipline to get up so early. He looked at me quizzically, and asked, "What discipline? It is my favorite time of the day!" He went on to say if he *did* wake up at 3 a.m. saying to himself, "I *have to* get up because it is so *good* for me. I *have* to keep my weight off. I *must* lower my blood pressure," he would find a hundred very good reasons for *not* getting up, and he would stay in bed. He went on to say that when he does wake up, his first thought is how beautiful it will be on the top of that hill, where he can see the stars above and the city lights below. So at 3 a.m. every morning, he puts on his running shoes, dons his iPod Shuffle, drives over to the hill, and starts running up; again, not because he has to, but because he wants to enjoy his favorite time of the day.

I mentioned earlier how at one time in my life I taught college during the day and then served as Evening Dean at night. I basically worked from 8 a.m. until 9 p.m. One night while leaving the campus at 9:30 p.m., a student who had seen me during the day asked how long I had been there. I replied that I had arrived at 7:45 a.m. that morning. He then exclaimed, "Isn't that hard?!" My response was automatic, no thinking required: **"Not when you love what you are doing!"** *That* is constructive motivation.

Making Your Mind Your Motivator: Part II

When we began looking at constructive motivation, I said that there was also a second option: **"You must accept the consequences of your decisions."** Let's look at that now.

The statement, **"You must accept the consequences of your decisions"** has a very portentous ring to it. In fact, it can also be expressed as **"You *have to* accept the consequences of your decisions...or else!"**

Oops! We are back to the have-to's and restrictive motivation again! We have already learned that bringing any have-to's into your thinking is like waving a very red flag in front of a bull—

your mind reacts immediately by sitting up on its haunches, and exclaiming, "Oh, yeah! *Make me!*" This is then followed by procrastination, creative avoidance, or slovenly work...not the best partners for change.

Instead, let's consider an alternative to, "You must accept the consequences of your decisions." One which works very effectively is this: **"You *get to enjoy the benefits* of your choices."** We have made three changes here, and each one converts the statement from a have-to to a get-to...from *restrictive* motivation to *constructive* motivation. Let's briefly consider each one.

"You get to..." rather than *"You must..."*

We have already learned that beginning a sentence with "You must do so-and-so" or "You must *not* do so-and-so" makes your mind want to *do* so-and-so, or *not* do so-and-so. That's the way we're wired. It is the same as being told to *not* think of a red-faced monkey when your eyes are closed, or being specifically told that there is absolutely no fishing from the hotel balconies in Galveston, Texas. This is the reason that sentences beginning with "You must" or "You have to..." or "You should..." are usually self-defeating.

We replaced "You must..." with "You get to..." This motivates your mind to accept the changes you are making in your life. Rather than exclaiming, "Oh, yeah! Make me," it anticipates those changes. Why? Because *getting* to do something is far more motivating than *having* to do something.

"Enjoy..." rather than *"accept..."*

The word "accept" can have a very ominous ring to it. It means "to agree or consent to" and is often associated with things you do not *want* to accept. As we have discovered, your mind reacts against this through procrastination, etc. The word **enjoy,** however, has the opposite affect. Your mind becomes your motivator.

"The benefits" rather than *"the consequences."*

The word **"consequences"** has the same menacing feel to it as the words **You must** and **accept**. Nothing more need be said.

Applying Constructive Motivation to Your Affirmation

So how can you apply constructive motivation to your affirmations? Actually, it is deceptively simple. Simply look at each one and ask the question, *"Why* do I want this change in my life?" If the answer involves a "have-to," or a "should," or a "must," you know you are using *restrictive* motivation, not constructive. Your mind will in turn not be much of a motivator. You then need to take the second step described below in the examples:

> **Example One: I enjoy imprinting my affirmations daily because it is so easy and fun.**

This certainly has the correct form and format. However, if your incentive *behind* this affirmation is if you don't imprint these affirmations, then reading this book will be a waste of your valuable time, you are using restrictive motivation and your mind will not be of much of a motivator. A second step is then necessary, and that is to focus in on the positive changes you will be seeing in your life.

> **Example Two: I love arriving at my job on time with an open mind and positive attitude**

This also has the correct format. Again, though, if your incentive *behind* this affirmation is that you *have to* arrive to work on time or else you'll get fired, you are using restrictive motivation and your mind will not be much of a motivator. Just like my pushing on your hand, you push back. A second step is then necessary, and that is to focus on the benefits you are enjoying by arriving to work on time. These might be peace of mind, learning how to get up earlier, or learning how to be more disciplined with your time.

Example Three: I love weighing only 140 pounds because it makes me feel so great about myself.

This also has the correct format. However, if the incentive is that you *have* to or *should* lose (or gain) weight, the motivation is still restrictive and your mind will not be there to motivate you. So you need to take that second step by switching the focus from your *having to* lose weight to the benefits of weighing less (or more) These might include better feelings about yourself, lower blood pressure, and having a positive relationship with your bathroom scale.

Next Chapter Preview

We have just discovered that your mind can act as your motivator for change when you have the right *motivation: Constructive motivation.* However, this book has not yet answered a critical question: Even with the discoveries of how your brain learns, and how your self-images are formed, and how important goals are, and how to create affirmations, and making sure you have the right motivations, can you *permanently* change the way you think? Can we really switch our motivations from have-to's to get-to's…or from *restrictive to constructive*? In other words, can we go from having *pessimistic* tendencies to *optimistic* ones?

Happily, we can. In fact, one of the most significant findings in psychology in the last 40 years is that we can indeed choose the way we think.[86]

In the next chapter then, we will narrow our focus on a particular field of psychology that contrasts optimism and pessimism. So hang on to your hats; we still have so much more to learn.

Remnants to Remember

- Restrictive Motivation
  - Contains the words "Have-to," "Need-to" and "Must" and usually ends with the words "Or else."
  - "You have to accept the consequences of your decisions."
- Constructive Motivation
  - I don't have to meet my goals, I want to meet them.
  - I like what I am becoming, and I love what I am doing...
  - ...and they are my idea
  - "You get to enjoy the benefits of your choices."

Points to Ponder: Changing Your Affirmations from Restriction to Constructive

Let's now look at your motivations *behind* the affirmations you created in Chapter Fifteen. To do so, rewrite each affirmation you wrote in the space provided, followed by what you think and feel is your motivation *behind* that affirmation. If it contains such phrases as "have to" or "must" or "need to" or "should," it is probably restrictive. If it *is* restrictive, you are on your own in terms of changing yourself. Your mind will not provide much energy or creativity for change. If your motivation *is* restrictive, rewrite it as a constructive one in the space provided.

Affirmatio

_____

_____

_____

Write your motivation behind this affirmatio

_____

_____

If your present motivator is restrictive, rewrite your motivator so it's constructive.

_____

_____

_____

Affirmatio

_____

_____

_____

Write your motivation behind this affirmatio

_____

_____

If your present motivator is restrictive, rewrite your motivator so it's constructive.

_____

_____

_____

Affirmatio

_____

_____

_____

Write your motivation behind this affirmatio

_____

_____

If your present motivator is restrictive, rewrite your motivator so it's constructive.

_____

_____

_____

CHAPTER NINETEEN:

How to Change the Way You Think

• •

Jaws Revisited

Steven Spielberg's movie *Jaws* may seem an odd place to begin exploring our capability to change the way we think. *Jaws*, however is considered one of the greatest cinematic masterpieces because of its concentration on the *characters*, rather than *the shark*. In fact, the shark itself has very little screen time. *Jaws* is about far more than a story of man defeating a shark; it is a chronicle of a particular man changing the way he thinks, and in turn changing *himself*.

As a review (if you have not seen it for a while, or were one of the astounding 69 million people who saw it when it was first released in 1975) *Jaws* is a fictional story about a series of shark attacks in Amity, a small beach community. Roy Scheider plays the main character, Sheriff Martin Brody. Brody lives on the beach with his family. Sheriff Brody, however, is less then the ideal 'hero' as reflected by the following dialogue involving his wife, Ellen.

Ellen: Martin hates the boats. Martin hates water. Martin sits in his car when we go on the ferry to the mainland. I guess it's a childhood thing, there's a clinical name for it, isn't there?

Martin: Drowning.

For Martin, living right on the beach is like a visitor living in a foreign land. In the last third of the movie, however, he leaves the safety of his house and enters a sea defined by lawlessness and a survival-of-the-fittest mentality. The fact that he *leaves* his house reflects a man who *must* change, and in the end, does. At the very end of the movie, *he* is in the water fighting one-on-one with the shark. He defeats the shark. Why? Because he *can and did* change his thinking. He did so by summoning the courage and strength to win.

So let's learn how this can be done!

It Began in the 1960s...

As little as 40 years ago, peoples' behavior was assumed to be a product of their environment. The Freudians believed that unresolved childhood conflicts drove our behavior as adults. The behaviorists held that all of our behavior was based on "external reinforcement." The ethologists believed it was totally in our genes, and the evolutionists believed that our actions were based on the need to reduce our drives and satisfy our biological needs.

The 1960s, however, brought far more to history than the flower-children of San Francisco. It brought a radical change on how psychology viewed human behavior, with the more dominant theories shifting to an individual's capability to *chose, decide,* and *control*. In fact, for the very first time in history, due to an explosion in neuroscience, we have learned far more about how our brain works in the last five years alone than since the dawn of man. With the advent of computer technology, the explosion of information through the Internet, the fall of the Berlin Wall,[87] and other reasons, we now know enough about how our mind works for people to gain control of not only how they think, but their own lives as well.

One of today's pioneers of psychology is Dr. Martin E. P. Seligman. His more than 20 years of research about learned optimism has formed a significant foundation for this book; we will be touching on some of the highlights he has discovered in this chapter.

Pessimism vs. Optimism

According to Dr. Seligman, these two habits of thinking can be defined by how people react when things happen in their lives.

For instance, when good events happen to *pessimists*, they:

1. *Temporalize* them
    - "Yes," they say. "What has happened is indeed good. But wait until tomorrow! The good never lasts. My life will be the pits again!"
2. *Isolate* them
    - "Yes," they agree. "This part of my life has turned out pretty well, but that is only because I was lucky. The rest of my life is really awful, or really bad, or really depressing."
3. **They believe they deserve none of the credit.**
    - Pessimists believe that they have nothing to do with anything good that happens to them. It is all "luck," or "chance," or in the "stars."

When good events happen to *optimists*, however, they react differently. They:

1. *Eternalize* them
    - They are not surprised when good things happen. "Of course!" they exclaim. "Good things usually happen to me. And even when they are bad, I have learned how to make them good, or see the good in them."
2. *Globalize* them
    - When good things happen to optimists, they are not surprised, for they believe that *most things* in their lives are good.

3. **They believe that *they* did it.**
   - Optimists are not afraid of taking credit for the good things that happen to them.

Now let's look at how pessimists and optimists react when *bad* things happen to them.

When "bad" events happen to pessimists, they:

1. *Eternalize* them
   - Their belief is that a bad or negative event is simply one of many that has always been happening in their lives, and that they are helpless to prevent. They believe that bad events will always be their "lot in life."
2. *Globalize* them
   - When bad things happen to pessimists, they believe everything in their lives is bad, "So why am I not surprised?"
3. **They believe it is all their fault**
   - Pessimists usually carry around a tremendous and unnecessary burden of believing that the sole reason for all the woes in their life, and perhaps in the world…is them! I have had grown adults tell me that they "knew" as children that all the children in such-and-such a country were starving because these adults had not eaten their peas when they were little.

Finally, when "Bad" events happen to optimists, they:

1. *Temporalize* them
   - "Yes," they say. "My life is really hard right now. This event is awful, and it will take me a while to get out of it. It may take me a few months to pay off this debt, or perhaps a few years. But someday it will be paid off. Things won't always be this bad."
2. *Isolate* them
   - "Yes," they agree. "This part of my life is really hard, or awful, or difficult. But everything in my life is not

bad. These parts over here, in fact, are very good, or healthy, or moving in the right direction."

3. **They believe it is *not* all their fault**
   - Optimists do not allow themselves to carry all the blame for bad things that happen to him. They have realized how they are just fooling themselves by assuming that they alone are the source of all their problems.

It's More than Whistling a Happy Tune

Although it may seem that pessimism is permanent in the way a person views the world, years of psychological research has shown that pessimists *can* become optimists.[88] However, this transformation does not take place through simply whistling a happy tune, or mindless platitudes ("Every day I am getting better and better…") or trying to blindly think positively. Your mind won't be fooled by that.

The change takes place when we learn how to think *differently*, as we have been learning in this book. Formerly this is called "cognitive thought" where 'cognitive' refers to the mental processes of reasoning, in contrast to the emotional highs you get from listening to an inspirational speaker, or thinking that if you just think positive, everything will be OK.

There are two key elements that need to be understood in order for the affirmations you created in Chapter Fifteen to become permanent. They are wrapped up in:

- Your self-talk
- Your beliefs about what happens to you.

But First, A Word of Caution

Learning to be optimistic must be approached with caution. While optimism does have some outstanding virtues (which we'll see in a minute), a question arises that we must address: Does my learning how to be optimistic mean that I must also sacrifice being realistic?

Absolutely not!

We will not be suggesting an absolute, no-holds-barred, unconditional optimism that blindly accepts everything that happens to us with half-opened eyes. We are offering a **flexible optimism**: One which can release you from, as Dr. Seligman expresses it, the "tyranny of pessimism." When misfortunes strike, we will learn in this next section how we have a *choice* about how we can look at those misfortunes. And we will also see that we have discovered alternatives.

Contending with Cancer

As I was leaving the college one afternoon, the front receptionist beckoned me over to her desk and said that my wife Mary was on her phone. I took her phone to hear Mary tell me she was just walking out of our doctor's office.

"I have breast cancer."

Everything within me stopped. Along with our daughters and their husbands, we gathered at our house and talked...and ate...and cried...and drank...and laughed.... and ate some more, and then regrouped.

We knew that Mary would take the next few months off of school (she is an elementary school principal) and endure all that fighting cancer entails.

It was then that I asked myself, "How can I apply what I have been teaching to something like this?" I realized that if I could not, I really should not be teaching it!

It is the "Learned Optimism" from this chapter that helped us the most.

During our talks into the night, we decided to have three perspectives. We would *isolate* the cancer, we would *temporalize* it, and we would emphasize that it is *no one's fault*.

Isolating Cancer

Although cancer and its treatment are very hard to endure, we decided to isolate it in our lives. This does not mean we pretended it was not there (you cannot do that with cancer). However, we concentrated on other parts in our lives as well: our children, our love for each other, our living in Sonoma County, my being a college professor. Although the song "Count Your Blessings" may seem a bit trite, its message is the same. Yes…the affect that cancer has on our bodies is horrible, and fighting it is also very hard, but it was not the only thing in our lives. There were others that we fastened onto, just like the boy on his bike fastens onto the rock in the road. And this helped us tremendously.

Temporalizing Cancer

We also said to ourselves, "This cancer is temporary. Someday, Mary will not have cancer anymore. There will be an end to this." And we took that vision and brought it into our present…NOW! We looked to the day when there would be no cancer…no more surgeries…no daily trips to the radiation clinic…no daily sickness…the treatment would be over…Mary would be back in school. That became our mind-set. It did not change the possibility of cancer someday returning, but it changed our feelings, and made it a bit easier for Mary to endure the treatments.

It is not my fault!

When Mary first discovered her cancer, she was her own worst enemy for the first couple of days. "Oh…if I had eaten more healthy food…or exercised more…or drank more water…I would not have gotten cancer. It is all my fault!" But over time we saw that cancer simply happens, just as sickness does, and there is no one to "blame!" There is no "shame" or "guilt" in cancer. It just occurs. When we ask ourselves, "Why me?" the answer is invariably, "Why NOT me?" What makes me so special that I should not get breast cancer? Millions do.

It Goes Back to Your Self-Talk

Learning to be optimistic is not a rediscovery of the "power of positive thinking." It does not consist of simply saying positive things about everything. In fact, in the decades that Dr. Seligman and his colleagues have been doing their research and working with their clients, they have found that simply making positive statements to yourself has little, if *any,* effect.[89] What is crucial is what you say to yourself **when you *fail*.** In fact, changing all those destructive messages we often give ourselves after experiencing setbacks is the *central skill* behind learning optimism.

One Bible verse reads, "It rains on the just...and the unjust." To illustrate, I talk to my students about the difference between being younger and being older. When younger people plan something that does not happen as planned, they get very surprised. However, when older people plan something and it *does* happen as planned, they get just as surprised. Why? Because the older we become, the more we learn that planned events seldom work out as we thought they would. Life inflicts the same setbacks and tragedies on all of us, whether we are pessimistic or optimistic.

However, studies have repeatedly demonstrated that optimists recover faster. Professor Madelon Peters, along with his colleagues at Maastricht University in The Netherlands, has shown that optimistic people and those who are less scared before an operation often have fewer pain complaints after a year, function better, feel more recovered, and experience a higher quality of life.[90] In another study[91] from the *Journal of Personality and Social Psychology,* researchers surveyed 99 men at age 25 and rated their degree of optimism about life in general. Doctors then examined these men at age 65 and found that the optimists had survived middle age in better health.

All of this would be bad news if pessimists were doomed to always be pessimistic. However, they are not. You *can* indeed learn to be more optimistic by simply learning a set of skills about how **you talk to yourself** when you suffer a personal defeat.

Let's examine that now.

Our Beliefs about Life Events

Most of us connect how we feel with events in our lives. If good things happen to us, we feel happy and satisfied. If bad things happen to us, we feel sad or mad. As a result, we spend our time and energy attempting to rearrange our *circumstances* in order to insure our happiness. The fly in the ointment is those people who are in *miserable* situations and are completely happy and content. We have also met people who are in *wonderful* situations to die for, and literally wish they could.

This dichotomy suggests that our emotions and behavior are *not* dependent on what is going on around us. We can buy that brand new car we have always wanted, or acquire that 'perfect' job, or develop a relationship with that "wonderful new someone," or finally lose that 50 pounds, and still find ourselves feeling not quite right, or worse. This happens because something else is going on, something that determines how we feel. This additional factor is our thoughts or belief systems.[92] According to the American psychologist, Albert Ellis, one of the originators of cognitive-behavioral therapies, it is in fact, **your self-talk**! Albert Ellis is considered to be the second most influential psychotherapist in history (Carl Rogers placed first in the survey; Sigmund Freud placed third).[93] Ellis originated what he called the ABC's of our emotions[94] which we will now briefly consider.

> The "A" represents your circumstances ("A" stands for **A**ctivating Events), including everything going on in your life, and "C" represents your feelings, which Ellis refers to as "Emotional **C**onsequences."

Now…our natural tendency is to think that our activating events (A) determine our emotional consequences (C). In other words, A=C.

For example, if an activating event (A) is that Johnny does not return Shirley's phone call, the emotional consequences are that she feels hurt and rejected.

So, A is followed by C

Other examples could include:

*I got a D on my test (A), so I really **feel** stupid. (C)*
*Sally didn't invite me (A), so "Boy, do I **feel** ugly." (C)*
*I'm still too overweight (A), so I will **always** feel fat. (C)*
I didn't get a raise (A), so I feel horrible about my job. (C)
He won't stop yelling at me (A), so he makes me feel so angry! (C)

You could then write countless other examples into the parentheses: $A(\ ) = C(\ )$.

Wait a minute! What happened to the "B?" The B is our beliefs, as verbalized by our self-talk. And B *always* comes between the A and the C. In the same way, our self-talk *always* comes between the circumstances and the resulting feelings.

David Stoop has his Ph.D. in clinical psychology and is the founder of *The Center for Family Therapy* in California. He has diagrammed this relationship as follows:[95]

Activating Event (A) causes	Beliefs (Self-Talk) (B) which causes	Emotional Consequences (C)
I got a D on my test.	I must be really stupid!	I feel really stupid!
Sally didn't invite me.	It must be because I am ugly.	Boy, do I *feel* ugly.
I blew my diet this week.	I *must* never blow my diet.	I'll always be overweight.
I didn't get the raise.	I must be doing a horrible job.	I feel horrible about my job.

As we can see from this diagram, it is not the activating event that causes our feelings; it is what we *tell ourselves* about the event that causes our feelings. Another way to say this is that it is *beliefs* about those circumstances that do the damage.

Albert Ellis expresses it this way:

"It is not our life events (Actions) that themselves, directly disturb us (produce unpleasant emotional consequences). It is our irrational demands, our shoulds, druthers, and musts (Beliefs) that largely do the job.[96]*"*

So let's return to the previous examples, change the beliefs, and look at the results.

Activating Event (A) causes	Beliefs (Self-Talk) (B) which causes	Emotional Consequences (C)
I got a D on my test.	1. I didn't study enough. 2. I didn't understand the material. 3. I didn't get enough sleep the night before.	1. I'm not stupid, I'll just study harder next time. 2. I'm not stupid, I'll meet with the professor to be sure I understand the material better next time. 3. I'm not stupid, I'll just go to sleep earlier next time.
Sally didn't invite me.	1. She doesn't like me anymore. 2. Maybe she just forgot. She does have a lot of friends.	1. That will make me sad for a while, but I have other friends. 2. That makes me feel bad, but not about myself. I myself have forgotten to invite people to my own parties. All of us do make mistakes.
I blew my diet this week.	1. No law says I must never blow it. 2. It's completely under-standable that I would be upset at myself. 3. I am not worthless because I screwed up. 4. One failure does not mean total failure. 5. This simply assumes that I must be thin, and although I would like to be thin, I don't have to be.	1. The next time, I will eat more slowly/ take smaller helpings/ drink more water. 2. I'll let myself feel bad for a few minutes, and then I'll let…it…go. 3. This does not affect who I am. After all, today is a new day. Today is a new "start-over." 4. I'm still learning this new pattern of eating and exercising. 5. I am comfortable with myself no matter how much I weigh.
I didn't get the raise.	1. I am working as best I can. 2. The economy is not conducive to raises right now. 3. Missing a raise does not mean I am a bad worker.	1. As I am working as best I can, I feel comfortable when I leave work. 2. I still have a job. 3. I am still a valuable person.

What did we just do? We adapted a discipline called the Three Minute Therapy[97] as developed by Dr. Michael Edelstein, Ph.D. It involves six simple steps:

A. Identify the **A**ctivating Event that has caused your feelings. ("I have lost my job.")

B. Now identify the **B**eliefs you have about those activating events. ("I *must* be a useless person if I don't have a job!")

C. Feel the emotional **C**onsequences. ("I feel useless as a breadwinner and horrible about myself as a person.")

D. **D**ispute those beliefs, especially the "musts." Are they really true? ("Am I really a useless person if I don't have a job?" Absolutely not!)

E. Develop a new more **E**ffective and reasonable way of thinking. ("In the present economy, hundreds of thousands are losing their jobs. However, not having a job does not reflect my value as a worker or as a person.")

F. A new **F**eeling then arises. ("Although I don't have a job right now, I know I eventually will, and this gives me the confidence I need as I search for a new job.")

How Does This Apply To Affirmations

Why learn this after you have created your affirmations? Because in order for affirmations to really work, you *must* understand that it is NOT the circumstances in your life that determine how you feel about yourself. It is what you *tell* yourself about those circumstances that do (i.e., your self-talk).

This is the psychological reason that affirmations must be directed to your self-talk. A misunderstanding of this is one of the primary reasons why affirmations do not work for a lot of people. They direct their affirmations at their *feelings*, and think that by simply repeating them over and over, their feelings about themselves will change. When this does not happen, they become very discouraged and depressed and simply resign themselves to returning to their old ways. But affirmations were *never* meant to change your feelings about yourself. They change how you *see* yourself.

Next Chapter Preview

We have learned that our feelings do not always come from events around us, but our *beliefs* about those events. And we also have learned the steps to change those beliefs. However, what do you do when you blow it? What do you do when you take a step backward, or two or three? How do you keep on track when you gain that weight back, or lose your temper again, or say things you didn't mean, or still seem to be late all the time?

This question must be answered because we are the most vulnerable when we *do* blow it. So we'll learn how to handle that in the next chapter.

 Remnants to Remember

When Bad Things Happen

Pessimists	Optimists
1. They globalize it: *Everything* is bad. 2. They eternalize it: It will *always* be bad. 3. "And it's all my fault…"	1. They isolate it: *Everything* is not bad. 2. They Temperalize it: It will not *always* be bad. 3. "And it's not all my fault…"

When Good Things Happen

Pessimists	Optimists
1. They isolate it: *Everything* else is bad 2. They temperalize it: It will only be good for a while. 3. "I had nothing to do with it…"	1. They globalize it: Everything is good. 2. They eternalize it: It will always be good. 3. "And I did it!"

Points to Ponder:

1. Would you describe yourself as more of an optimist or a pessimist? Why and why not?

_____

_____

_____

_____

_____

_____

_____

_____

CHAPTER TWENTY:

What to do When You Blow It

• •

Life Just Gets in the Way

When asked why 40 percent of the students at the University of Phoenix dropped out of college, Dr. William Pepicello, the University president, gave two reasons in a cnn.com interview. The first was financial. The second, he said, was that *"life just gets in the way."*[98]

Although what we have so far learned can make such a difference in our lives, we must also address what to do when *life gets in the way.* In other words, what about the times when we must take some steps backward, or we want to give up, or we *have* to give up? If we don't address these, this book will merely be another inspirational work that eventually ends up as a bookend on your shelf.

We learned in the last chapter that our feelings come from our beliefs, not what happens to us; although many of these beliefs are very deeply rooted, many are also very false. It is for this reason that we are ready to probe a bit deeper to see where they came from. You and I both know that merely believing that "your life will be fine" does not make your life fine. This kind of thinking runs along the same vein as the glib advice, "Don't worry, be happy!" However, our affirmations *can* work even while life is throwing all it does at us. To understand this, let's now turn to our own *system of beliefs.*

It Begins with Your Belief System

When asked to look at their *system of beliefs,* many people have pronounced that they no longer *have* a system of beliefs. They exclaim that it is just too hard to believe *anything* anymore because people "just can't be trusted." And yet our entire life is based—it *must* be based—on a system of beliefs. The fact that you are sitting on a chair, or drove in a car today, or rode on a bus yesterday, testifies to your belief that the person who assembled that chair made it sturdy enough for you to sit on, or that car sound enough for you to drive, or that bus is safe enough for you to take. In fact, our entire life *must be* based on our belief systems. If it wasn't, you would spend the day cowering in your bed. (Even then, you would still have a belief system that your bed had been built sturdily enough to hold you.)

As we examine some of our faulty belief systems, we will discover that living in the 21st century has given us a significant advantage over our ancestors. Through the work of tens of thousands of neuroscientists, and such psychologists as Albert Ellis, Michael Edelstein, David Steele, Martin Seligman, and thousands of other therapists, we now have a far better idea of how our brains and belief systems work. Let's begin looking at your belief system by contrasting evaluations and preferences.

Evaluations and Preferences: Contrasted

Virtually all of our feelings come from personal evaluations. For instance, a statement such as "Dr. Smith is my personal physician" is simply a fact, with no evaluations or feelings attached. However, "I am *glad* that Dr. Smith is my personal physician" is more than a fact; it is an *evaluation*, and this evaluation causes feelings. So, "I *regret* that Dr. Smith is my personal physician" or "I *love* Dr. Smith being my personal physician" are all evaluations, and all of these trigger feelings.

Some feelings obviously are quite strong, others not strong at all. In fact, the strength or feebleness of your feelings can be theoretically scaled, where 0 percent means that you have no feelings at all about Dr. Smith being your personal physician, to 99.9 percent[99] where you feel that "Dr. Smith *must* be my personal physician or you feel that you will absolutely *die!*" The feelings which land around the middle of this theoretical scale are called **preferences;** you could describe these as "appropriate and reasonable." For instance, "I like Dr. Smith being my personal physician" is a certainly appropriate and reasonable. In contrast, "Dr. Smith *must* be my personal physician or I feel I'll absolutely *die!*" seems rather extreme. It is close to the top of the scale, and is no longer "appropriate and reasonable." In other words, preferences can become **demands** when their strength reaches the top. When this happens, the "musts" and "shoulds" can cause some problems.

Back to the Musts and the Shoulds

Although we have already looked at these when we considered *restrictive motivation* in previous chapters, we are now ready to look at them a bit deeper. Not only are "musts" and "shoulds" and "have-to's" a form of restrictive motivation, they can also be called "demands." For example, one of the greatest fears of college students is to give a presentation in front of other students. They often say to themselves, "I must be outstanding, because if I reveal how little I know about what I am presenting, I know I'll just die!"

All of these are "demands," and we make them all the time. Other examples include:

1. **"I *must* not look foolish when I do my presentation!"**
2. **"I *must* not embarrass myself."**
3. **"I must look great!"**
4. **"I must lose 10 pounds by January 31 or I'll always be fat!"**
5. **"I must get an A or I'll feel really stupid!"**
6. **"I must get a raise or I'll feel *totally* worthless!"**
7. **"I must not get sick because getting sick means I'm weak!"**
8. **"I must have the perfect wedding because that's what we deserve!"**
9. **"I must have the perfect marriage because we love each other so much."**

It is also helpful to know that in addition to the demands we place on ourselves, there are three other types. They include:

1. The demands we place on others. (He *must* like me or they *must* agree with me.)
2. The demands we place on situations. (I *must* not lose my job or I *must* earn such-and-such a salary.)
3. The demands we place on the universe. (It *must* not rain or The weather *must* stay perfect.)

As you look at these demands, you begin to see that they are simply notions that have become commands we make on ourselves, on others, or on life itself. Most of them also have a magical ring about them, because their origin is usually a mystery. So if someone asked you, "Who said so?" you would be hard pressed to find an answer. But even though their origin remains unknown, they can lead to self-defeat, anger, anxiety, and self-pity. When taken to the extreme, they can also lead to such problems as violence, addictions, gambling, and compulsive shopping.

A Key to Healthy Thinking: Preferences are Preferable

A key to healthy thinking is to realize that having preferences, even strong preferences, is perfectly normal. It is one of the traits of being human. However, turning them to demands puts undue stress in our lives. In fact, the majority of emotional problems arise when individuals believe that something or other MUST be, or not be.[100] With this in mind, let's look back at the "musts" that we listed above and see what can happen when we change them to *preferences*.

1. **Rather than "I *must* not look foolish when I do my presentation!"**
   - "I don't want to look foolish, but my life will not end if I do. And the more I make presentations in front of other people, the more comfortable I will become doing it."

2. **Rather than "I *must* not embarrass myself."**
   - "I have embarrassed myself before, and although I felt very uncomfortable, I lived through it, and even laughed at myself in the end."

3. **Rather than "I *must* look great!"**
   - "I would like to look great, but I don't need to be the center of attention tonight. And I know I'll look really nice."

4. **Rather than "I *must* lose 10 pounds by January 31 or I'll always be fat!"**
   - "It would be nice to lose 10 pounds my January 31, but even losing less would be quite an accomplishment."

5. **Rather than "I *must* get an A or I'll feel really stupid!"**
   - "It would be gratifying to get an A after all the work I've done, but that grade doesn't reflect how smart I am or my intelligence."

6. **Rather than "I must get a raise or I'll feel *totally* worthless!"**
   - "A raise would certainly help us right now financially, but I won't allow not having a raise affect how I see myself. I'll try to find out *why* I didn't get it, and either improve my work, or consider other options."

7. **Rather than "I must not get sick because getting sick means I'm weak!"**
   - "I would prefer not getting sick, but everyone does... including me. If I *do* get sick, I'll do everything I can to get well, but I'll also enjoy the time off."

8. **Rather than "I must have the perfect wedding because that's what we deserve!"**
   - "Of course I would love to have "The perfect wedding," but that is simply unreasonable, and the emotional cost of striving to make it perfect can make me, and everyone around me, miserable. So I'll concentrate on having a great wedding, and leave the 'perfect' out of it."

9. **Rather than "I must have the perfect marriage because we love each other so much."**
   - We *do* love each very much, but we are also two individuals who are learning the joys and hardships of sharing our lives together, and our marriage will reflect both of those.

It seems that the purpose of changing demands to preferences is to protect you from having *unrealistic* or *unreasonable* goals. So rather than saying, "I *must* get an A," you should think more realistically by saying, "It would be gratifying to get an A after all the work I've done, but that grade doesn't reflect how smart I am or my intelligence." *But wait a minute!* Doesn't that return us to the danger of the "How" question we discussed in Chapter Seventeen? Not at all! In fact, preferences do the very opposite. Let's see how by looking at the result of changing the demand, "I must get a raise or I'm no good!" to the preference, "A raise would certainly help us right now financially, but I won't allow not having a raise affect how I see myself. I'll try to find out *why*

I didn't get it, and either improve my work, or consider other options."

The demand, "I must get a raise or I'm no good" is a dead-end street which leaves you no wiggle room. Either you get the raise or "you're no good." A preference, however, opens up other options to you, such as:

1. I won't allow not having a raise affect how I see myself.
2. I'll try to find out *why* I didn't get it.
3. I'll either improve my work, or I'll consider other options.

In other words, when you view your goals as preferences, rather than demands, they add motivation, they add passion, they add challenge, and they add the burning desire to keep growing. Rather than your mantra being, "I'm not good because I didn't get the raise" it becomes "The next time (remember that way back when?), I won't allow not having a raise affect how I see myself." Or, "The next time I'll find out why I didn't get it." Or, "The next time I'll improve my work." Or, "The next time, I'll consider other options."

What to Do When You Blow It

You now have the resources to deal with the times you blow it, or when you become discouraged because your affirmations are not working quickly enough, or the demands you place on yourself are wearing you down. However, *using* these resources is another thing, so let's learn the steps now. We'll use Denise as an example.

Denise's Current Situation

Denise has been working at her company for about a year. Last month, the president of the firm asked her to give a monthly PowerPoint presentation on various subjects he will assign. Although Denise gave presentations as a college student, she has *never* spoken in front of any other group, much less a group of architects and is scared to death!

Denise's Affirmation:

> "I am so comfortable presenting in front of the architects in my office because I know they need to understand the subjects I will be presenting, and it is also an excellent way of marketing myself."

After reading *Making Your Mind Magnificent,* Denise wrote this affirmation for herself thirty days before her first presentation. She mounted it on her bathroom mirror, and for the first two weeks spent 30 seconds imprinting it into her mind every morning and every evening.

Denise's Restrictive Motivations and Resulting Demands:

> "This presentation *must* be perfect, or I just know they will not ask me to do another. I will also look foolish in front of the architects, and my job might therefore be in jeopardy."

As we learned in Chapter Seventeen, behind all of our affirmations are our motivations; either constructive or restrictive. You can tell that Denise is using *restrictive* motivations because they are based on fear, which you can see so clearly. The demand is "This presentation *must*...be perfect" and the restrictive motivators are, "I just know they will not ask me back," and I will look foolish" and "my job may be in jeopardy." After faithfully imprinting her affirmations for the first two weeks, however, Denise felt less anxious as the presentation approached. She then began skipping the morning imprinting session on the third week, and then some of the evening sessions on the fourth. She also eased back on her preparations.

When she finally gave the presentation, she walked out of the meeting feeling *very* bad about its quality, and the fact that the architects asked so many questions she couldn't answer. She felt that she had really blown it, and her self-confidence and fears about the future presentations put her in a downward spiral. Let's look again at the steps which Denise must take to get herself back on track. We learned these at the end of the last chapter. As you recall, they can easily be remembered by the letters ABCDEF.[101]

Step A: Identify the Activating Event:

The Activating Event was simply the presentation which Denise has been asked to do.

Step B: Look at your Belief about that event.

Denise's belief is wrapped up in the demand she has placed upon herself. "This presentation *must* be perfect!"

Step C: Look at your emotional Consequences

Denise's emotional consequences are expressed by, "I just know they will not ask me to do another. I will also look foolish in front of the architects, and my job might therefore be in jeopardy." Notice that the first and last of these beliefs are based on her fears, and nothing else. No one told her that she "will not be asked to do another," or that "her job will be in jeopardy."

Step D: Dispute your beliefs

As she returns to her desk after her presentation, Denise feels really down and defeated. This however, is the perfect opportunity to dispute her beliefs. Who said that "This presentation *must* be perfect?" Where did this belief come from?

A Word of Caution Here:

Does this mean that Denise should not evaluate her presentation to determine what she did right and what she did wrong? Absolutely not! Her feelings *do* tell her that she could have done better, and that is good. That is how we learn—through our mistakes. The problem is that we carry those feelings of failure around with us like a plague, and that is simply not necessary or healthy.

Step E: Effective New Thinking

While it is true that Denise could have done better, and she should have prepared more, no one told her that her job is not based on giving the "perfect presentation." This was simply an unrealistic fear she placed on herself. In fact, research has found that when people do makes demands on themselves, they then *imagine* the horrible things that happen if it they do not turn out. In Denise's case, however, this is the first time she has given a presentation outside of class, and she has many more to give. So her effective new thinking could be: "It would be great if the presentation was great, but if this first one is not, and I can learn from it and make a better one next time." In other words, there will always be a *next time*.

Step F: A New _Feeling_ arises

As a result of this new thinking, her self-confidence and fears about the future presentations were not affected.

A Question

Does this mean that it is "wrong" or "unhealthy" to feel a loss of self-confidence, or fearful when you do blow it? Absolutely not! That is also part of our being human. When this happens to my students, however, I give them the following advice.

1. Feel *really* bad about it...for no more than two minutes.
2. Learn what you can so it doesn't happen the next time.
3. Go through the ABCDE Steps as described above.
4. Follow this new feeling with "The Next Time...I Intend To..."

Two Steps Forward, One Step Back

When driving to the college where I taught for many years, my route was to stop at a light just before entering the freeway. There was a boy one morning in a huge SUV next to me. As we waited for the light to change, we glanced at each other, and I sensed his intentions to demonstrate the power of his SUV when the light turned green.

Sure enough, as soon as it did, he peeled out in front of me and roared up the freeway, apparently trying to get in front of everyone *else* as well. As I watched him race up the freeway, I was struck by an epiphany: How many cars are already in front of *him*: Thousands, even millions. And how many cars are also *behind* him: Thousands, if not millions. The *real* issue then is *not* when you get there, or whether you are doing *better* than someone else. The real issue is that you *are* getting there; per- haps at a pace which seems slower and a little wobbly at times, but getting there all the same. And you find yourself having to take two steps forward and one step back, but you *are* moving forward—you *are* changing those areas of your life you want to change…and your mind has indeed become…your motivator.

 # Remnants to Remember

We learned in this chapter that our feelings do not come from events that happen to us. They come from our *beliefs* about those events. This is wonderful to know, because changing our beliefs about events is decidedly easier than changing the events themselves. The steps to do that are as follows:

Step A: Identify the **A**ctivating Event.

Step B: Look at your **B**elief about that event.

Step C: Look at your emotional **C**onsequences.

Step D: **D**ispute your beliefs about that event.

Step E: **E**ffective New Thinking can follow by disputing your beliefs.

Step F: A new **F**eeling then arises within you about the event, and about yourself!

Points to Ponder

Einstein's wonderful definition of insanity is doing the same thing over and over and expecting different results.

So, in this Points to Ponder, write down four things you are going to do differently because of what you have learned from this book.

1. _____
_____
_____
_____
_____
_____
_____

2. _____
_____
_____
_____
_____
_____
_____

3. _____

_____

_____

_____

_____

_____

_____

_____

4. _____

_____

_____

_____

_____

_____

_____

_____

YOUR SECOND BENCHMARK

Making Your Mind Your Motivator—Bringing it All Together

You began this book to change how you see yourself, change some of the things you do, change some habits you have, and change *you*. You have discovered, however, that your mind often becomes your greatest obstacle. In fact, its job is to *keep* you from changing; to keep you in your comfort zone; to keep you where you are. And yet—and this is the enigma—your mind is the most satisfied, excited and creative when you *are* changing! In fact, it is the energy and creativity from your mind that enables you to change in the first place. However, as you have learned in this book, *you* must teach it this, for it does not *want* to change. Until just a few years ago, however, we did not know this. Now we do. When students ask me why no one had taught this years ago, I tell them we did not *know* this years ago, so this book could not have been written.

We must do far more then simply take away the mental obstacles our minds erect. We must teach them how to become our greatest motivators, our greatest supporters, and one of our dearest friends! And now that you have finished this book, you have the information to do that. However, as you know, having the information and knowing how to consistently use it are very different. In fact, all this knowledge and information can become easily muddled and confusing.

So, let's condense everything you have learned down to six principles you can put in your pocket and carry around with you. They can be divided into two groups:

1. Principles 1 through 3 review how to **create new self-images** that override the old.
2. Motivators 1 through 3 review the **motivators** that make those new self-images become permanent in your life.

Creating New Self-Images

Every one of the thousands of self-images you have was *learned*; you were not born with them. Most of them were based on three elements: What others said to you, how others reacted to you, and what you have said to yourself (i.e., your own self-talk). And as we have learned in this book, the brain accepts all of these unquestionably as the absolute truth.

But you now want more than that. You want to *choose* how you see yourself. You now want to proactively create your *own* self-images, rather than wait around for others to tell you who you are and what you can or cannot do. It is for this reason that what we believe about ourselves is far more important than you could possibly imagine. And it is also for this reason that all meaningful and lasting growth must start on the inside...with how you see yourself...with your self-images.

Let's again review the Principles that show us how.

Principle 1: Your brain is a literal mechanism that accepts what you tell it without argument.

This first principle is the foundation of everything that follows. In fact, if it was not true, the rest of this book would be useless. However, with every principle there are both positive and negative elements, the negative is that when you say "I can't do that!" your brain not only agrees, it blocks out possibilities *for* you to "do that."

That's the negative. When you say you *can* do something, your brain agrees just as quickly. Not only that, it also provides the creativity and the energy to get it done. The first step then to creating new self-images is to know this: Whatever you tell yourself about yourself and your capabilities, the brain accepts without argument.

Principle 2: Your brain fastens onto what you deem as important.

This is another principle of such importance that if it was not true, what follows would be no good to you.

My favorite story in this book (as you can probably guess by this time) is the one about the young boy learning to ride his first bicycle. If you remember, just before his father lets him go on his first ride, he points out a rock 50 feet ahead, and warns, "Now don't run into that rock!" The little boy agrees, and with his hands clinging to the handle bars, he begins peddling like mad with his eyes fastened on the rock so he won't run into it. And what happens? BAM! Right into the rock!

Our brains are the same way. Rather than the rock, however, our brains continually hone in on the pictures in your life that *you* deem as the most important. Our brains are like a guided missile continually correcting itself to follow that strongest target. And what are those targets? They are our own self-images. This is one of the many reasons why change is so difficult. Some of the strongest pictures in your life are the way you see yourself right now, wrapped up in the thousands of self-images you already have. In addition, these self-images are so wired into your brain that they can't be removed except through a pre-frontal lobotomy, which you definitely do not want. So for real change to occur in your life, you must find a better way.

That better way is to *override* them with stronger pictures which the brain will then follow. These "stronger pictures" are the affirmations you created in Chapter Fifteen.

Principle 3: Your affirmations override the self-images you want to change.

You created a number of affirmations at the end of Chapter Fifteen, and then learned the steps to imprint them. Imprinting them consistently over time then gives them so much personal value that your brain then fastens onto them, like the eyes of the little boy fastened onto the rock. Through these affirmations then, you are creating new self-images which then override the ones you no longer want as part of your life.

Making Your Mind Your Motivator

For this to take place however, having written affirmations is not enough. Your mind must then be brought over to your side. Remember, it is wired to resist most changes you want to make, no matter how healthy or good they may be. So simply knowing and practicing the steps for overriding your old self-images with new ones will not work over the long run unless your mind is working *with* you, and not against you. You *must* make it your motivator. So let's review how.

Motivator 1: Your affirmations cause a gap that your mind must close.

We began Chapter Seventeen by first learning about the inconceivable importance of goals: That without them, we die. We then learned that our brain needs order in its universe, and that all of us are working to maintain that order. By then coupling these two elements together, we learned how to create goals that cause a "gap," a gap which our brain then releases the creativity and the energy to close. And it is that creativity and energy from our minds that helps us reach our goals.

An affirmation is simply a personal goal written down. Let's imagine I have created an affirmation that says, "I *love* being consistently on time at work because it makes me more successful during the day." Now I created that affirmation because I have NOT been on time and I have not been successful. As a result, when I begin imprinting it, my mind sits up on its haunches and protests, "But you are *not* consistently on time, and you are *not* successful during the day!" This is the gap that it must now close. And it does so by first suggesting that I throw out the affirmation. "After all," it says, "you have always been late. Why do you think you will be any different? Let's return to the old self-image where you simply are a person that can never be on time. After all, that is your comfort zone. That is where you are the most comfortable...even though that zone is not good for you."

If, however, I keep imprinting this new affirmation; if I insist on making it a far stronger and more valuable picture, my mind will soon perceive its value and will fasten onto to it like the boy fastened onto the rock in the road. So, by creating that gap, my mind becomes my motivator!

It's for this reason that such goals as "I *will* quit smoking" or "I should lose weight" almost never work, because they give your mind no reason to change. Their response is simply, "That sounds good. It even sounds inspirational. But I deal with the present, not the future, so I see no reason to help you change. So not only are you on your own, I will resist your efforts to stop smoking or lose weight."

So, as we learned in Chapter Seventeen, your goals must actually create a problem your mind must then resolve, for it then has the incentive to change right along with you.

Motivator 2: Your affirmations are based on constructive motivation.

If I push against the palm of your hand with my own, you immediately push back. This is a direct reflection of what our brain is doing. When someone pushes on us, or we push on *ourselves*, we push back.

This ties into *restrictive* motivation. Restrictive motivation is almost always based on fear, and ends with the words "Or else." Goals based on restrictive motivation usually contain the words "have-to" or "must" or "should." Some examples might be, "I *have to* quit smoking because then I'll be healthy." Or "I *must* lose weight because then I will live longer." Or "I should spend more time with my wife because we will get along better." All of these are certainly true. However, when our brain hears the "have-to's" or the "musts" or the "shoulds," it pushes back as quickly as when you push back on my hand.

We learned in Chapter Eighteen how *restrictive* motivation can act as a death knell to most of our affirmations, because it causes us to push back, rather than move forward. *Constructive* motivation does just the opposite. Constructive motivation is based on the *value* of what you *want* to do, rather than what you *have to* do. It is a "get-to," rather than a have-to. You don't *have to* accept the consequences of your decisions, you *welcome* them. Your goals are then based on the following three incentives:

I don't *have* to meet these goals, I *want* to meet them.
I like what I am becoming, and I love what I am doing...
...and they are my idea.

With *restrictive* motivation, you must be willing to **accept the consequences** of your decisions. With *constructive* motivation however, you **enjoy the *benefits*** of your decisions. So, as you consider your goals and affirmations, make sure they are get-to's, not have-to's.

Motivator 3: Getting back up when we "fail."

We talked about the power of optimism in Chapter Nineteen. However, learning to be optimistic does *not* consist of merely saying positive things about everything. Research has discovered that trying to always make positive statements has little if *any* effect on our lives. What is crucial is what we say to ourselves **when we *fail***. In fact, changing all those destructive messages we often give ourselves after experiencing setbacks can become one of our greatest motivators.

So we learned in Chapter Nineteen how to change those destructive messages by first realizing that our emotions and behavior are *not* dependent on what is going on around us. We can buy that brand new car we have always wanted, or acquire that 'perfect' job, and still find ourselves feeling not quite right, or worse. The reason is that there is something else going on... something that determines how we feel. It is *not* the circumstances that cause our feelings; it is what we *tell ourselves* about the circumstances that do. Another way to say this is that it is the *beliefs* about those circumstances that can do the damage, especially when we fail. According to Albert Ellis, one of the originators of cognitive-behavioral therapies, this "System of Belief" is wrapped up in **your self-talk!**

So to change those destructive messages, especially when we fail, or when we must take a step back, we adapted a discipline called the Three Minute Therapy[102] as developed by Dr. Michael Edelstein, Ph.D. It involves the following five simple steps:

A. Identify the **A**ctivating Event that has caused your feelings ("I have lost my job.")

B. Now identify the **B**eliefs you have about those activating events. ("I *must* be a useless person if I don't have a job!")

C. Feel the emotional **C**onsequences ("I feel useless as a breadwinner and horrible about myself as a person.")

D. **D**ispute those beliefs, especially the "musts." Are they really true? ("Just who said that I am a useless person if I don't have a job? Is that true? Absolutely not!")

E. Develop a new more **E**ffective and reasonable way of thinking. ("In the present economy, hundreds of thousands are losing their jobs. However, not having a job does not reflect my value as a worker or as a person."

F. A new **F**eeling then arises. ("Although I don't have a job right now, I know I eventually will, and this will help give me the confidence I need as I search for a new job, and consider other healthy options to provide for my family while I don't have a job.")

And Finally...The Next Time...

The three most important words in this book are **The Next Time**...for it's these three words which make your mind your *greatest* motivator. It is these three words that stop you from giving up.

Why is this?

1. **There will *always* be another Next Time.**
   We have as many "Next Times" as we want. There *are* no limits. As long as we are alive, there can *always* be a next time; they *never* run out. That is why "The Next Time" is the mindset which great leaders take, and most of them have had to *learn* how to do so.

2. **Always Having a "Next Time" can be encouraging.**
   When you awake in the morning, you can say to yourself, "Great...I have another chance! I get another "Do-over." And having another chance means there is *still* room for learning and growing and changing.

And finally....

3. **"The Next Time" is a far healthier way to live!**
   The Next Time opens the possibility of new goals to you ...and reasons for you to keep growing and learning and changing.

This is why you have read this book—because of the passion which your mind has to grow. And now you know how to make it your greatest motivator...and companion...and friend.

You *will* do well!

Special Offer for Readers of *Making You Mind Magnificent*

For help on applying the latest brain research to your life, special offers, freebies, teleseminars, and my exclusive report titled "The Secret of Trading Your Past for What You Want Now," sign up for my newsletter at: http://www.stevenrcampbell.com/bonus

About This Book

This book costs $19.95. To purchase a copy, send a check for $24.00 (book price, plus postage and handling) made payable to "Steven Campbell" to:

Steven Campbell/An Intelligent Heart
P.O. Box 197
979 Golf Course Drive
Rohnert Park, CA 94928-2404

Please allow 2-4 weeks for delivery.

Special Pricing

For special pricing when purchasing 10 or more copies, please call: (707) 568-7322.

Steven in Person

Steven is available for speaking engagements, workshops, and individual consultations. To learn more, visit his Web site: www.AnIntelligentHeart.net or call (707) 480-5007.

About Steven Campbell

Steven Campbell is an author, speaker, and mentor to individuals and organizations worldwide. Making Your Mind Magnificent provides not only a simple yet comprehensive understanding of how your mind works, it also offers straightforward and easy-to-understand principles you can immediately apply to help you change the way you think.

Mr. Campbell acquired his Bachelors of Science Degree in Zoology from San Diego State University in 1970. He then worked for 18 years in administration in various California hospitals. After acquiring his Masters of Science Degree in Information Systems from the University of San Francisco, he went on to pursue his greatest love...teaching. He has been a college professor and educational dean in northern California for over 20 years. Mr. Campbell is also the author of two college textbooks published by Que Education and Training in 1998, and a third titled Making your Mind Magnificent, published in 2010. As well as being a radio host every Wednesday morning on KOWS (http://kows107-3.org/) for his world-wide program titled Making Your Mind Magnificent, Steven also conducts workshops throughout the United States on how to make our minds our greatest mentors.

To contact Steven or learn more about his workshops and other programs, please visit **www.stevenrcampbell.com**, or call 707-480-5007.

Endnotes

1 Feldman, R., _Power Learning, Third edition_ (New York: McGraw-Hill Higher Education, 2007.)

2 Cooper, R. K., _Get Out of Your Own Way_ (New York: Crown Business, 2006)

3 Hart, Leslie _Human Brain and Human Learning_ (Arizona Books for Educators 1983) 35

4 Hart, Leslie, p. 35

5 Drubach, Daniel, _The Brain Explained_ (New Jersey: Prentice-Hall, 2000)

6 Medina, John, _Brain Rules_ (Seattle, WA, Pear Press) 2

7 Medina, John, p. 53

8 Medina, John, p. 57

9 Kotulak, Ronald, _Inside the Brain_ (Kansas City, Andrews and McMeel, 1996) xii

10 Whalley, Lawrence, _The Aging Brain_ (New York, Columbia University Press 2001) 14

11 Haberlandt, K., _Human Memory; Exploration and Applications_ (Needham Heights MA: Allyn & Bacon, 1999)

12 Roach. J., Brain Study Shows Why Revenge is Sweet (_National Geographic,_ Aug. 27, 2004), available at http://news.nationalgeographic.com/news/2004/08/0827-040827_punishment.html

13 Holtz, R.L., Brain's 'God's Module' May Affect Religious Intensity," available at http://www.iol.ie/~afifi/BICNews/Health/health19.htm

14 See http://www.nimh.nih.gov/press/prworkalholicmonkey.cfm

15 http://www.neilslade.com/Papers/welcometoyourbrain2.html

16 http://www.neilslade.com/Papers/how.html

17 Luria, A.R., Frontal Lobes and the Regulation of Behavior in K.H. Pribram and A.R. Luria, Editors, (_Psychophysiology of the Frontal Lobes,_ New York, and London, Academic Press, 1973)

18 Lee Gomes, The Wall Street Journal, June 10, 2002

19 Hart, Leslie, p. 61

20   Hart, Leslie, p. 60

21   Hart, Leslie, p. 61

22   Smith, F., *Comprehension and Learning* (New York NY, Holt, Rinehart and Winston, 1975) p. 1

23   Hart, Leslie, p. 75

24   M.Le Poncin, *Brain Fitness* (New York: Ballantine, 1992) 65

25   Smith, F., p. 1

26   Jerison, H.J. *The Human Brain* (Englewood Cliffs, N.J.: Prentice Hall, 1977) 54

27   Hart, Leslie, p. 65

28   Hart, Leslie, p. 60

29   Hart, Leslie, p. 60

30   Hart, Leslie, p. 64

31   Bauer, J. *Joy's Life Diet*

32   Tice, Lou, *Thought Patterns for a Successful Career,* (The Pacific Institute, Seattle, WA) 46

33   http://www.my-inspirational-quotes.com/inspirational-stories/cliff-young-a-farmer-who-inspires-a-nation/

34   http://www.brainyquote.com/quotes/authors/h/henry_ford.html

35   Tice, Lou, p. 46

36   Tice, Lou, p.47

37   Cooper, R.K., p. 50

38   Dennis, J. *Money for Nothing* (Davison, MI, Friede Publishing, 1988)

39   R.B. Zojonc, Styles of Explanation in Social Psychology, *European Journal of Social Psychology* (Sep-Oct, 1989); J.L. Locke, *The De-Voicing of Society* (New York; Simon & Schuster, 1998); N. Nicheolson, "How Hardwired is Human Behavior?" *Harvard Business Review* (July-August, 1998); p. 134-147

40   http://entrepreneurs.about.com/cs/marketing/a/uc062003.htm

41   Tice, Lou, p.70

[42] Ellis, A. & Harper. R.A., *A Guide To Rational Living* (Chatsworth, CA: Wilshire Book Company, 1997) 66

[43] Tice, Lou, p. 22

[44] Ellis, A. & Harper. R.A, p. 66

[45] http://www.hvacprofitboosters.com/Tips/Tip_Archive/tip_archive7.html

[46] The Quotations Page," Accessed at http://www.quotationspage.com/quote/39852.html

[47] Tice, Lou, p.15

[48] Ellis, A. & Harper. R.A, p. xiii

[49] Tice, Lou, p. 70

[50] Tice, Lou, p. 89

[51] Stoop, D., *Self-Talk: Key to Personal Growth* (Grand Rapids, MI, Fleming H. Revell) 131

[52] Covey, S.R., *The 7 Habits of Highly Effective People*, (New York, Simon and Schuster)

[53] Aamodt, S. PhD, Wang, W. Ph.D., *Welcome to Your Brain (Bloomsbury, New York, N.Y. 2008) 2*

[54] Hart, Leslie, p. 64

[55] Tice, Lou, p.145

[56] Stoop, D., p. 45

[57] Tice, Lou, p. 31

[58] Tice, Lou, p. 32

[59] Cooper, R.K., p. 19

[60] Cooper, R.K., p. 22

[61] Kennedy, P., *The Rise and Fall of the Great Powers*, (New York: Vintage, 1989)

[62] Sull, D. *Revival of the Fittest* (Boston Harvard Business School Press, 2003) 45-48

[63] Collins, J. *Good to Great* (New York, Harper Collins Books)

[64] Amunts K., Kedo O., Kindler M., Pieperhoff P., Mohlberg H., Shah N., Habel U., Schneider F., Zilles, K., <u>Cytoarchitectonic mapping of the human amygdala, hippocampal region and entorhinal cortex: intersubject variability and probability maps.</u>" Anatomical Embryology (Berl) 343-52

[65] Cooper, R.K, p. 22

[66] LeDous, J. *The Emotional Brain* (New York,: Putnam, 1997)

[67] Cooper, R.K, p. 88

[68] Einstein, A. *Ideas and Opinions* (New York: Wings, 1988)

[69] Stoop, D., p. 47

[70] Tice, Lou, p. 113

[71] Tice, Lou, p.113

[72] Tice, Lou, p.114

[73] Cooper, R.K, p. 1

[74] Cooper, R.K, p. 5

[75] Stoop. P. p 30

[76] Stoop. P. p 31

[77] Stoop. P. p 49

[78] Tice, Lou, p.163

[79] Tice, Lou, p.172

[80] Cooper, R.K, p. 9

[81] Helmstetter, S. PhD *What To Say When You Talk To Yourself* (New York, New York, Simon & Schuster, 1982) 34

[82] http://seniorjournal.com/NEWS/Retirement/5-10-21Retire55.htm

[83] Tice, Lou, p. 194

[84] Assaraf. J & Smith, M. *The Answer: Grow any Business, Achieve Financial Freedom, and Live an Extraordinary Life* (New York, N.Y., Simon and Schuster, Inc.) 71

[85] Medina, J., p. 112

[86] Seligman, M.E. PhD, *Learned Optimism: How to Change Your Mind and Your Life* (New York, N.Y., 1990) 8

[87] Friedman, T. *The World is Flat: A Brief History of the Twenty First Century* (New York, N.Y., Holtzbrinck Publishers, 2007)

88 Seligman, p. 5

89 Seligman, p. 15

90 http://www.unimaas.nl/rESEArChmaGazIne/default.asp?id=1
85&thema=5&template=thema.html&taal=en

91 http://www.medicinenet.com/script/main/art.
asp?articlekey=50849

92 Stoop. P. p 28

93 *New York Times: Despite Illness and Lawsuits, a Famed
Psychotherapist Is Temporarily Back in Session* (December 16,
2006)

94 Stoop. P. p 28

95 Stoop. P. p 30

96 Ellis, A, & Harper, R.A. *A Guide to Rational
Living,*(Chatsworth, CA: Melvin Powers Wilshire Book
Company, 1997) 57

97 Edelstein, M. PhD, *Three Minute Therapy,* (Aurora, CO,
Glenbridge Publishing Ltd, 1997) 208

98 http://business-degree-online.bestmanagementarticles.com/
Article.aspx?id=992

99 You can never prefer something at 100% because you can
theoretically always feel stronger about something

100 Edelstein, M. p. 7

101 Edelstein, M. p. 7

102 Edelstein, M. p. 208

Made in the USA
San Bernardino, CA
30 December 2018